Santa Cruz Beach Boardwalk

The Early Years — Never a Dull Moment

By
Chandra Moira Beal
and
Richard A. Beal

First Edition

Cover design by Lyn Bishop, Zama Online Design (www.zama.com). Book formatting by Jackie Iddings (www.jackieiddings.com).

Cover photograph of the rebuilt casino courtesy of the Museum of Art & History@The McPherson Center, Santa Cruz, California. Back page photograph of bathing beauties courtesy of University of California Santa Cruz Special Collections Library. The Plunge interior photograph courtesy of Harold J. Van Gorder Collection. Title page photograph of Ray and Margaret McCullough courtesy of Noni Borden.

While all the information in this book has been carefully researched, neither the authors nor the publisher assume any liability for errors or omissions in the actual content of the book.

 Printed in the United States of America on recycled paper.

Publisher's Cataloging in Publication

Beal, Chandra Moira and Richard A.

    Santa Cruz Beach Boardwalk: The Early Years – Never A Dull Moment

p. cm.

Includes biographical sketches of early characters

Includes biographical references

Includes index and bibliography

ISBN 0-9629974-2-0

Table of Contents

Forewords

Chandra

After I wrote my first book, *Splash Across Texas! The Definitive Guide to Swimming in Central Texas*, people immediately began asking me when I would write my second book. I tossed around ideas for a few years, but it wasn't until my father, Richard, suggested the history of the Santa Cruz Beach Boardwalk that I was inspired.

The Boardwalk holds magical memories for me as I know it does for many Santa Cruzans, native and visitor alike. I remember the anticipation of growing tall enough for my first ride on the Giant Dipper, trying to stretch as tall as I could to pass the mark. I recall being mesmerized by the salt-water taffy pull, having my fortune told in the penny arcade, and watching the Monterey Bay shrink below from the top of the Ferris wheel.

As a child, the Boardwalk was a very special destination, a place we only went to for birthdays or significant events. In my teens, the Boardwalk was a place to hang out on warm summer nights, giggling and waiting for friends to finish their shifts. And today, it is still a place we take visitors from out of town, or sneak in a lunchtime ride on the Dipper to relive those magical moments of childhood.

While researching this book, I was struck by how the Boardwalk represents the essence of Santa Cruz. The progress of the Boardwalk mirrors the city's development into a thriving resort destination, the spirit of entrepreneurism, and the population's perpetual sense of being on vacation. Learning about the area's history was fascinating, and strengthened my heart's connection to this wonderful town and especially the Boardwalk.

Santa Cruz is a magical place that has been blessed by nature. Our bodies may age but the Boardwalk keeps us young at heart. The wonder and joy of childhood live on at the Santa Cruz Beach Boardwalk.

Richard

My first historical book, *Highway 17: The Road to Santa Cruz*, sold over 35,000 copies and ignited my interest in learning more about our local history. In searching for another popular topic that holds a special place in the hearts of many residents and visitors, the Santa Cruz Boardwalk became an obvious choice.

My father Ralph (Chandra's grandfather) visited the Boardwalk in the 1920s as a small child, but my first visit wasn't until 1975. I'm sorry to say I'd never even heard of the Boardwalk before moving to Santa Cruz. One of the first weekends there, I took my then six-year-old daughter Chandra and her three-year-old brother Andrew to the Boardwalk, primarily because it was free!

Over three million people visit this small spot on earth every year, parents often bringing their children so they can pass on their own happy memories from years past.

What is the attraction? The Boardwalk is always the same and that is part of its charm, but it continues to bring a few new attractions every year that give us an excuse to return. It is safe, it is slightly old-fashioned and quaint, there is excitement, laughs, and of course the beach - a great place to stroll. There are literally dozens of things for people to do at the Boardwalk, from the corny to the memorable, from the heart-stopping Giant Dipper roller-coaster to the nostalgic carousel. You can relax, just walk and people watch – or you can go full out and do every ride and visit every concession and eat some junk food along the way. Just think how many photographs have been taken at the Boardwalk over the past 99 years!

Why write this book? Because the Boardwalk is a microcosm of the history of the wonderful city of Santa Cruz. Tourism has always been our most important local industry and the Boardwalk has been the largest attraction. The Boardwalk is also one of the county's largest employers. No history of Santa Cruz could be written without telling of its role in making what we see in today's city.

I am excited when I see the old historical photos and feel a personal link to the past. I want to picture what those people were like, how their days went, what they did, how they felt.

Join us as we go back in time together. Get your bathing suits and the suntan lotion. Let's go to the Boardwalk!!

P.S. The real blessing of his book has been co-researching and writing it with my daughter. Thank you, Chandra, for making this such a wonderful experience. I'm so proud of you!

Note To Historians

This book is incomplete. We feel that we simply opened up some of the early Boardwalk history and attempted to provide an overall historical framework and timeline for what we hope will be many future books and articles by other writers. This is a rich area for historical research.

Unfortunately the Seaside Company that owns and manages the Boardwalk does not allow historians general access to their archives of documents and photographs, so much of the original source material is not available.

In this book we relied heavily on newspaper articles of the time, UCSC Special Collections Library materials, and, where possible, interviews with still-living local residents who have recollections of the times. The Santa Cruz Museum of Art and History archives also proved to be a valuable source of information. Special thanks to the Friends of the Santa Cruz Library volunteers who continue to index early newspaper articles. Without them the book could not have happened.

We do want this book to be accurate so if you notice any errors please let us know. You can contact us at la-luna@att.net or PO Box 33189, Austin, Texas 78764.

The Early Beach Years

From the very beginning, Santa Cruz's scenery, and especially its beaches, played a central role in the town's development. This is the story of the heart of Santa Cruz, the beaches and people that created the Santa Cruz Beach Boardwalk.

Santa Cruz, California is nestled between the Pacific Ocean and the Santa Cruz Mountains, perched at the northern tip of Monterey Bay, and 75 miles south of San Francisco.

The modern history of the town began in 1542 when Spanish explorer Juan Rodriguez Cabrillo visited the area inhabited by Ohlone Indians, probably landing on the same beaches that would later provide the town with its main source of revenue and identity. In 1792 an adobe mission was constructed on what later became known as Mission Hill and the town began to develop in the small valley below the church.

Santa Cruz was described by French Captain Duaut-Chilly, who visited during the mission days: *"There is no more beautiful situation than that of this Mission. Leaving the shore the land rises in terraces so regular that one would imagine them the earth works of a fortification. I doubt even, if by clothing them artificially with turf, we could ever arrive at the beauty of the greensward that covers them like the carpet of green velvet which is stretched on the steps of a throne."*

Santa Cruz's central location on the West Coast made it a major shipping port for raw materials and agricultural products during the 1800s, and the town's natural beauty attracted many visitors. In 1862, the San Francisco Bay Association held its convention in Santa Cruz to escape the Civil War activity and mobilization in the city. Convention-goers returned with glowing reports of Santa Cruz's scenery, a first inkling of the city's resort potential.

The City of Santa Cruz was incorporated on March 31, 1867, but getting to Santa Cruz in the early days was no picnic. Visitors had to travel all day over the mountains on undeveloped dirt trails, usually on horseback or by stage, until 1881 when the first regular train service began from Watsonville (which connected to the rest of the San Francisco Bay area).

Nineteenth-century residents and visitors alike found Santa Cruz a charming and idyllic resort. With the Santa Cruz Mountains framing the town and hugging it against Monterey Bay, and the San Lorenzo River flowing from the mountains to meet the Pacific Ocean, the scene was ripe for opportunities in recreation and tourism. Later a 20th century postcard produced by the Chamber of Commerce proclaimed Santa Cruz "The Riviera of the New World" and "The Playground of California and the North Coast Convention City." Over the years Santa Cruz was also advertised as the "Switzerland of America," and the "Atlantic City of the Pacific," emphasizing the redwood groves, mountains, lodges, and beaches.

Plate I ~ Early days before the Boardwalk existed. [Courtesy of The Museum of Art & History@The McPherson Center, Santa Cruz, California]

Despite its natural beauty, Santa Cruz lacked the sharp contrast of San Francisco's hills and rugged coastline, and its beach promenade was somewhat monotonous. In the 1860s, there were very few buildings on the shore. Only a few ships were anchored in the bay, and the commercial wharves were uninteresting to tourists.

"With the exception of the climate, there is but little in the village itself to charm that cannot be found in a thousand other villages. Only a few of the main visitors to Santa Cruz become at all acquainted with its genuine attractions. These are on the hills and in the woods, upon which it seems to us God has put more of thought than upon ordinary scenery." ~ *Santa Cruz Sentinel*, May 21, 1864

The bay teemed with life then as it does today. Tide pools full of sea anemones, starfish, sand dollars, crustaceans, and all manner of shellfish enchanted people who came from the interior parts of California and further east.

Plate 2 ~ The lower plaza about 1860. One of the oldest known pictures of Santa Cruz. Hugo Hihn's Flatiron building (center) was just completed. Lower left corner, Elihu Anthony's building from 1847; on "the flat" beyond: the Santa Cruz House, Franklin House, Saloons, Chinese Laundries. Lower right: Charles D. Endon's store; beyond, Frederick A.A. Hihn's store. The beach where the Boardwalk will be built is on horizon in the picture. [Courtesy of the Harold J. van Gorder Collection]

The typical summer beach scene in the late 1800s could be described as an outdoor Elysium. Aquatic birds such as pelicans and sea gulls floated lazily on the water. Seaweed, or sea moss, collected on the sand. Locals could always pick out tourists because they stopped to gather the abundant sea moss. Children and babies

Plate 3 ~ Muddy streets in downtown Santa Cruz. Front Street on the left, what is now Pacific Avenue on the right. [Courtesy of the Harold J. van Gorder Collection]

played in the surf, while sails of fishing boats glinted in the sun. Colorful, striped umbrellas dotted the sand, protecting tourists from the sun. Horse-drawn carriages passed up and down on the sands, and a fresh salt breeze caressed the beachgoers. A visit to the beach was a highly social affair with couples and families promenading down the sand in their best clothes. In fact, there was a 1904 ordinance requiring men on the beach to wear a coat and hat. The local newspaper published lists of families who had established tents at the beach or who were seen swimming and sunning.

"It is well known that Santa Cruz has long been a favorite resort for those desiring the luxury of a good sea bath; the beach affords superior facilities for bathers, not equaled by Brighton, Newport, or any other fashionable resort. The bathing grounds extend along the sandy beach about one mile from Davis & Jordan's wharf to the estuary formed by the junction of the San Lorenzo River, which place is at present the location of bathhouses, and where parties daily resort for purposes of bathing and enjoying a delightful swim, either in the salt, sea, or the fresh limpid streams, clear as crystal, and pure as when it leaves the towering hills." ~ *Santa Cruz Sentinel*, June 3, 1865.

Plate 4 ~ Beach area in the 1880s. [Courtesy of the Harold van Gorder collection]

A typical party held in June 1884 was described in the newspaper as:

"Santa Cruz beach was never more delightful and attractive than last evening and even the habitual beachgoer could not resist the exhilaration of the scene. The broad expanse of the beach was never cleaner, finer, or more charming as a boulevard or a promenade.

The cordial good will of the people towards the 'Grand Army' of veterans was manifested by the thronging crowds that moved beachward at nightfall on cars, in busses, private conveyance, and in the more primitive but not less pleasurable manner, as pedestrians. The members of W.H.L. Wallace Post are to be congratulated upon the success of their entertainment last evening for even that fickle goddess 'California climate' smiled upon them and rolled back the curtain of foggy clouds which had obscured the day, and revealed all the glories of moonlight on the water. A merry throng filled the seats and the sands. In front of both bathhouses soon after dusk, enjoying the soft air, the flash of the breakers and the music of the Pythian Band, stationed on the balcony of the bathhouse. The supper tables were spread at the Leibbrandts' while the Neptune, decorated with evergreens, flowers, and national colors, was devoted to dancing. At the appointed hour the crowd drew to the water's edge, where they greeted the coming of Neptune and his attendants as per program. They drew near upon a barge illuminated by colored lights and greeted from the shore by bonfires.

"Neptune was evidently somewhat unaccustomed to that mode of conveyance as he or one of his followers lost his equilibrium and tumbled into the water. However he was soon right side up and reaching the shore the party was escorted to the dancing hall by a guard of the G.A.R., the water gods, seeming rather abashed in the presence of so many mortals and modestly tying to hide their blushing countenances. The

Plate 5 ~ Unknown friends pose in front of the bathhouse (before the Casino). [Courtesy of The Museum of Art & History@The McPherson Center, Santa Cruz, California]

dancing hall filled up rapidly soon becoming almost too crowded for comfort. After midnight the tables at the Leibbrandts' were cleared away and dancing went on there. The supper, consisting of delicious sandwiches, cake, and coffee, was gotten up by the ladies of the G.A.R., and ice cream was also dispensed with fair hands, Mrs. Peakes receiving the prize for selling the most.

"Outside the bathhouses people lingered till a late hour, watching the moon as she rose in splendor flirting to their heart's content and having a generally social time."

Nature endowed Santa Cruz with resources for becoming the most delightful place for residence and resort on the western shores of the American continent, and it had commercial advantages sufficient for the development of a large and prosperous business community. Despite general agreement that Santa Cruz had significant tourism potential, no one had yet proposed any sort of serious development in that direction. The town persistently and successfully foiled attempts to build grand hotels such as those found in the east or in Europe.

"It is true that the people of Santa Cruz have steadily shut their eyes to its opportunities," wrote a resident to the *Santa Cruz Daily Surf,* the local newspaper. *"While in the past the effect of this practice may have been only to retard and delay its development, the time is coming, yes, and now is, when this stubborn blindness will result in closing the door of opportunity against this town for all time to come. Santa Cruz should be the coast outlet for that mighty area known as the San Joaquin Valley."* ~ *Santa Cruz Daily Surf:* February 15, 1892

Plate 6 ~ Downtown Santa Cruz. Looking down Pacific Avenue (the street on the right) towards the beach. [Courtesy of the Harold J. van Gorder Collection]

Traffic began to increase between California ranches as agricultural products were distributed around the country and materials were shipped to and from the coast. California needed a coastal outlet to serve the interior of the state. Monterey and San Luis Obispo were added to the Southern Pacific line, but Santa Cruz still lacked rail service. Concerned that Santa Cruz might be eclipsed by other towns for lack of appreciation or opportunity, citizens deliberately set out to make theirs one of the finest stretches of ocean beach in the world, and the premiere watering place of the California coast.

Plate 7 ~ Horse trolley lines down Pacific to the beach. [Courtesy of the Harold J. van Gorder Collection]

As luck would have it, America experienced a bathing craze in the 1880s. The recent discovery of germs and the importance of preventing the spread of disease spawned a new interest in cleanliness and health, and people began washing daily. Hundreds of resorts and hot springs popped up around the country attracting thousands of people seeking to "take the waters." Reminiscent of ancient Rome, some springs were part of elaborate resorts that provided entertainment and recreation. Towns such as Hot Springs, Arkansas; Sulphur Springs, West Virginia; Saratoga Springs, New York; and Mineral Wells, Texas earned fame for their "magic water curatives."

Sea bathing had a draw all its own. Some claimed that sea bathing was good for you because it generated electricity, and the skin absorbed phosphorous and salt. One Santa Cruzan, writing from personal experience, recommended plunging into the rollers just as they were breaking to obtain the greatest amount of friction to create electricity. He advised bathers not to dry off but to let the salts be absorbed into the skin. To test this, he said, *"One need only take a bath on a dark night and rub the body briskly, and witness a glow similar to the phosphorus seen on a wall after striking a match." ~ Santa Cruz Daily Surf:* April 11, 1889. The next day a letter from a physician appeared in the newspaper refuting this, stating there was no basis in fact for these claims. Whatever the case, people were fascinated with sea bathing.

Plate 8 ~ Horse-pulled trolley on Pacific Avenue and Sycamore Street around 1885. The trolley connected downtown Santa Cruz (top) and the beach area. [Courtesy of the Harold J. van Gorder Collection]

Plate 9 ~ 1893 beach area where the Boardwalk will be built. The area just past these buildings is a shallow marsh that is commonly flooded by the adjacent San Lorenzo River or beach high tides. The dark roofed building closest to the trolley says "free museum." The Neptune Baths were built opposite where the trolley is. [Courtesy of Covello and Covello Collection]

Bathing costumes began to develop to accommodate the new craze. In those days women were well covered up, and even glimpsing the outlines of a person's body was nothing short of scandalous. As ladies left the dressing room to walk to the beach, all movement was hidden by clothes and a tall wooden fence. They wore long-sleeved blouses with a high neckline, stockings, and sandals. All suits had bloomers that reached to the knees. Added to this ensemble were hats with wide brims pulled down over the face and ears.

A few young women gave up the use of veils or parasols to sit in the blaze of the sun to get what théy called an "oxidized tanning," a novel idea at the time reputed to hide freckles. To protect their complexions while swimming, some women wore a mask of chamois leather with embroidered lips and eyebrows. Other girls wore padded bathing suits so as to *"enable the wearer to display dimensions where dimensions are most lacking. They are considered a great public benefit." ~ Santa Cruz Daily Surf:* July 18, 1883

One man wrote to the newspaper after admiring two female beauties on the beach that eventually decided to brave the surf. When he saw them dripping wet in their layered costumes, he was aghast at how the seawater had stripped them of their beauty, all their ornaments gone.

"While at the beach the present week, I beheld a shameless man. He came from the bathhouse, his bathing suit fitting so tight as to show every muscle and vein in his person. In the midst of the large gathering he stopped and viewed himself conversing at the time with a second man I shall not say gentleman. Sitting about were ladies and young girls, and I unhesitatingly pronounce the bather's dress as vulgar in the extreme. If your authorities and public sentiment do not insist on common decency along the waterfront the beach will be given over to indecent people. Signed, Mother." ~ Letter to the Editor, *Santa Cruz Sentinel*, June 23, 1883

Men wore calceons, one-piece bathing suits that came down to the knees or sometimes the feet, resembling an undershirt above. Most swimsuits were black or navy and trimmed in black or white tape. Daring swimmers wore red suits. Most suits were made of cotton, some of poplin, and a few were silk. And then, some people wore nothing: *"There are a large number of men and boys, full-grown Hoodlums, who daily trespass on our Bay, by going in swimming, near the wharf of Davis & Cowell, without bathing suits on. This practice should be discontinued, as many ladies and children are daily on the Beach and are driven away by the rudeness." ~ Santa Cruz Sentinel:* September 13, 1873

Although the pleasure of swimming is as old as the history of man, swimming as we know it today didn't exist at the time. Strokes had not yet been developed, and most people did not know how to survive in the water. During the Victorian age, swimming was associated with sensual pleasure and was discouraged. Swimming was a novelty.

More and more people were coming to Santa Cruz to sea bathe, but the Pacific waters were too cold for most. They needed a first-class resort to take advantage of the fabulous beaches, and facilities for bathing in style.

The Wharves

Santa Cruz originally had four wharves. The very first was Elihu Anthony's wharf, built in 1853. This wharf came down at an angle from a cliff at the end which is now Bay Street, which allowed trams to descend with barrels of lime to the level of the decks of small schooners tied at the end.

Davis & Jordan bought Anthony's wharf in 1855 and rebuilt it to serve steamers. This wharf later became known as the Cowell Wharf when Henry Cowell took over Davis & Jordan's business. Cowell used his wharf to ship gunpowder in 1863. He then built a new wharf off of Main Street on Beach Hill that was known as the Pacific Coast Steamship Wharf for the ship it served. The Cowell wharf collapsed in 1907 during high seas.

David Gharkey's wharf dated from 1857. It was also designed to serve the railroad. In 1875 Gharkey's was acquired by the South Pacific Coast narrow gauge line as a stop on the way to and from Los Gatos. Gharkey's was sometimes called the fisherman's wharf. It was in use until 1922, eight years after the present Municipal Wharf was built.

The California Powder Works built their own wharf in 1865, jutting over today's Main Street. The company had a plant on the San Lorenzo River where today's Paradise Park is located. In 1877 the Powder Works and the railroad built a connecting pier between their wharves to permit movement of freight. It proved impractical and flimsy and was removed after five years.

The Early Bathhouses – Liddell's

Several bathhouses populated the beach long before the Boardwalk was built. The first of these was probably the Long Branch Baths, opened by Mary Liddell in 1864. After divorcing Captain Timothy Dame and gaining custody of their son, Alfred, Mary moved in with her mother, Elizabeth. To earn extra income, they turned their one-story Beach Hill home into a boarding and bathhouse with a waist-deep seawater pool. These were the first hot saltwater baths west of the Mississippi, and a welcome alternative to swimming in icy Monterey Bay. The following year they built dressing areas covered with a canvas roof on each side of the bathhouse.

Plate 10 ~ Posed picture showing beach fashions. Ladies unidentified. [Courtesy of The Museum of Art & History@The McPherson Center, Santa Cruz, California]

Plate 11 ~ Horses and buggies on the beach long before the Casino is built. The steam-driven merry-go-round is on the left. Two sets of tracks, one for the train, one for the trolley. Advertisement for "The Surf Best Paper" (*Santa Cruz Daily Surf*), restaurant, and museum signs. [Courtesy of the Harold J. van Gorder Collection]

Plate 12 ~ Horse-pulled trolley. Beach is on the right, train tacks to the right of the trolley. [Courtesy of the Harold J. van Gorder Collection]

Plate 13 ~ Greeting the arriving train. Tourists, hotel representatives, and locals greet the arriving train before there were cars. [Courtesy of the Harold J. van Gorder Collection]

Another bathhouse, called Sweeny's, opened near Liddell's. One morning a serious accident happened when a large iron boiler, holding 1,650 gallons of water under full steam pressure, fell and demolished the walls of the brick work enclosing the furnace. Mr. Sweeny had been on the top of the furnace and tank, some 12 feet high, but luckily escaped a few seconds before it fell. Heating water by steam was the preferred method in those days, but it didn't come without its dangers.

> "Liddell's gives 6 swimming lessons for $3." ~*Sentinel*, July 7, 1879

Other bathhouses cropped up around the mouth of the San Lorenzo River, but Liddell's flourished. Many of these bathhouses offered only simple bathtubs, but they also rented swimsuits, umbrellas, and beach tents to enhance visitors' beach experience. Freshwater baths were offered alongside seawater baths, and both in a variety of temperatures. Santa Cruz began to build its reputation.

The Leibbrandt Brothers — The Dolphin Baths

By far the most successful bathhouse on the beachfront property was operated by the Leibbrandt Brothers and what they built became the springboard for the future Boardwalk. The Leibbrandts were early German settlers who came to Santa

Cruz in 1863 and operated a large farm on the beachfront between Cliff Street and the San Lorenzo River. The sons, John, Jake, and David, lived with their elderly father. Johnnie and David were both avid swimmers and regular competitors in the Santa Cruz to Capitola open water competition. Together they built the West's first hot saltwater plunge, a much larger swimming pool than the existing baths. The Plunge opened in 1868 just east of today's Neptune Kingdom. The Leibbrandts named it the "Dolphin Baths," and their facility featured a large pool and a fine ballroom upstairs. A steam generator pumped in saltwater straight from the ocean and heated it for bathers' pleasure. The same generator doubled as the power source for a steam-powered calliope at poolside.

Plate 14 ~ Leibrandt Brothers Dolphin Bath House, 1888. John Jacob Leibbrandt is on the extreme left, to his right is swimming instructor Bill Daily, John and Jacob Leibbrandt, and other employees. [Courtesy of University of California Santa Cruz Special Collections Library]

The Leibbrandts anchored wooden rafts offshore where swimmers could sun or rest in between dips in the water. The rafts were popular but had to be replaced periodically because of the wear and tear they suffered out in the breakers and in occasional storms. Swimming from the shore to the raft became the test of endurance for beginner swimmers. The brothers hired "natatorial artists," or swimming instructors, to teach their guests how to float, stroke, and get the most out of their bathing experience.

The Dolphin Baths were a resounding success. By 1873, thousands of people were flocking to the baths year-round, especially in the summer. At the height of the season, an estimated 1,000 people took the baths each day, which brought in enormous profits.

In 1885 they hosted "the best of local celebrities, Hawthorne, Hannah and Uhden, an array of talent from abroad; Burnett and Jordan of the Olympic Club, Hobbs of San Francisco, and the brothers Bacon of Alameda."

The Leibbrandts also held swimming and diving exhibitions and competitions. In October 1875, an open water swimming match was held between B. Gardner of the Ocean View House and John Leibbrandt for a purse of $100. Whoever swam the longest would win the money. The contestants struck out South towards Soquel and after proceeding about two miles, Johnnie suddenly sank from exhaustion. William Daily, his trainer, was close by in a boat. He dove in and brought the sinking man to the surface. At this time Gardner was at least 400 yards in the lead, and was declared the victor. The event marked the onset of debilitating arthritis for Johnnie and he was bedridden by 1887. He never fully recovered and eventually died from his near drowning experience.

Plate 15 ~ Beach before the Boardwalk. Swim dive platform anchored in the water, rented umbrellas. [Courtesy of The Museum of Art & History@The McPherson Center, Santa Cruz, California]

The Leibbrandts' business thrived. They constantly enlarged and improved their establishment and furnished more and more bathing suits in order to accommodate their increasing customer base. They began to host dances, build restaurants, hold parades, and give concerts. With Fred Swanton they built Dolphin Park across the street from the baths in 1897 and sponsored a baseball team, the Beachcombers. The Dolphin became a major social destination in California. Word began to spread about Santa Cruz's fabulous baths, and its reputation attracted investors hoping to copy the model with similar properties. Sensing competition, the Leibbrandts began buying up the other riverside bathhouses and property.

Plate 16 ~ Pre-boardwalk era. Temporary tents shelter picnickers and decorated visiting ships anchored out in the bay. [Courtesy of The Museum of Art & History@The McPherson Center, Santa Cruz, California]

Plate 17 ~ Before the Casino. Courtesy of the Harold J. van Gorder Collection]

Wheaton's Bathhouse

In 1879, a "gentleman of means" by the name of A.F. Wheaton arrived in Santa Cruz from the East. Seeing the success of the Dolphin Baths, and hoping to invest his money in a similar enterprise, Wheaton decided to build a large-scale bathing establishment where today's Casino stands. Wheaton's vision was to build a bathhouse that would provide "that completeness which tends to the comfort of the patrons—people of refinement and taste." Wheaton began construction on a $12,000 resort midway between the powder mill wharf and the Dolphin Baths. A skilled architect was employed and the building contract was let to L.B. McCormick, a well-known contractor and builder in Santa Cruz, who immediately set to work on construction. Shortly after the framework was up and the building partly enclosed, a whirlwind caused the building to fall flat to the ground. The carpenters barely escaped with their lives. However, work was immediately resumed and the wreck repaired, and within a few days the structure was completed.

Wheaton's bathhouse was an ample 40 x 100 feet and two stories tall. There were 100 separate bathrooms with all the modern improvements. One of the main features of the building on the lower floor was two plunge baths, separated by a partition for each gender. Each pool measured 14 x 25 feet with a depth of two to seven feet. Wheaton ordered 300 bathing suits for his patrons of "the newest and best material." Three separate steam pumps, with a pumping capacity of 15,000 gallons per hour, were kept constantly at work keeping the three tanks on the top of the roof full, as well as filling the swimming baths. One of the pumps was filled with fresh water, while the other two contained salt water, one being heated by steam.

Wheaton's facility also offered bathtubs for those desiring more privacy, made of galvanized iron with wooden bottoms. The bathrooms were said to be superior to any in the state. The upper floor of the bathhouse contained a refreshment saloon where visitors could obtain "any of the substantial" for a small cost. There was also a large 60 x 40 dance hall, well lit by windows on either side and well-ventilated with a 16-foot high ceiling. Adjoining the dance hall was a bar room and men's hat and dressing room. Two broad, covered verandas ran the entire length of the building.

Wheaton also built a large awning on the front of his building where patrons could sit in swings or at tables and watch the surf from the shade. He moored a raft offshore with a springboard in competition with the Leibbrandts.

Plate 18 ~ About 1876, Pacific Avenue horse car and Santa Cruz & Felton railroad passenger car at Gharkey's Wharf terminal. The Boardwalk will be built to the left of his picture. Cowell Wharf partly visible on the right. Structure at left had several names during its 100 year life: "Sea Foam," known as the Il Trovatore (destroyed by fire about 1907), operated by Peter Tori as a hotel, bar, restaurant, about 1930, and "Koinonea House" by a Christian community. [Courtesy of the Harold J. van Gorder Collection]

Plate 19 ~ Neptune Baths, pre-1906. Notice all the horses and buggies. [Courtesy of The Museum of Art & History@The McPherson Center, Santa Cruz, California]

Plate 20 ~ Before the Casino. [Courtesy of the Harold J. van Gorder Collection]

Many splendid hotels were built to accommodate the increasing number of visitors to Santa Cruz. Grand places such as the Pacific Ocean House on upper Pacific Avenue, Douglas House, Swanton House, and Kittredge House hosted visitors staying in Santa Cruz for weeks or months at a time. A horse-drawn buggy took visitors from the train depot to the hotels. Guests were surrounded by luxury, their rooms decorated with redwood and velvet. They had flower gardens for strolling, restaurants with local cuisine, balconies with ocean views, and all the modern amenities of the time. Hotels held grand balls and suppers for their guests, many who were spending their days at the bathhouses.

By the 1880s, other amusements began to appear around the bathhouses. Local businessman F.A. Hihn converted a skating rink into a dance pavilion. In those days, people came to the beach for

> Pacific Avenue was originally called Willow Street, but the name was changed in 1866 so tourists would know which street led to the ocean. ~ Margaret Koch, Author/Historian

extended periods of time because traveling was slow and arduous. The socially elite stayed at the grand hotels such as the Pacific Ocean House. Others could rent a tent on the beach for $10 a month. The price included four pillows and three logs to use as back rests.

Plate 21 ~ In front of the Neptune baths pre-1906. [Courtesy of The Museum of Art & History@The McPherson Center, Santa Cruz, California]

Beach Street as we know it today didn't exist in the 1860s, so carriages drove right onto the sand. The Leibbrandts built the original Boardwalk in 1868, consisting of rough-hewn wooden planks and railroad ties, to improve access to their baths. In 1876 they laid a gravel foundation and later railroad tracks were built over the stone. The fill dirt on the sides eventually evolved into Beach Street. In 1885, work began on a 12-foot-wide planked walk laid flush with railroad ties, funded by the city. The walk extended from the Douglas House to the Neptune Baths.

The Miller Brothers — The Neptune House

Captain Fred Miller bought out Wheaton's Bathhouse in 1885 and unified the two pools for mixed gender use. Fred and his brothers, Ralph and Albert, were Santa Cruz natives and sons of a sea captain. Fred was the youngest captain ever allowed to operate out of San Francisco. The family loved flowers and they planted yuccas (California Palms) and colorful flowers around the baths. They also built a long fence running from the ladies' apartments down to the watermark to protect their modesty. They applied fresh coats of paint throughout, and installed new sidewalks, elevating the Neptune to one of the city's finest bathing resorts, on par with the famous watering places of the east. But Fred Miller couldn't resist the call of the sea and he left in 1889 to become captain of the steamer *Maggie Ross*, leaving his brothers to manage the bathhouse.

Fred Miller's granddaughter, Florence "Chickie" Mills, recalled that her grandfather improved upon the bathhouse, but that her grandmother actually ran it because Fred was away at sea most of the time. Two years later, Chickie's father, Captain James Mills, also a sea captain, settled down ashore. He and his wife took over the Neptune. They lived upstairs from the baths, and Chickie was put to work cleaning showers and dressing rooms and renting out bathing suits. In those days, women paid 25 cents for a complete beach ensemble that included a corset, long stockings, bathing suit, garters, kerchief, and a straw hat. Men's suits were the same price unless they wanted the long-legged union suits that covered the feet. Those were 50 cents. Children were charged 10 cents to use the bathhouse if they brought their own suits and towels.

Plate 22 ~ Pacific Avenue horse trolley and the Neptune Baths, 1891-1892. [Courtesy of the Harold J. van Gorder Collection]

Across from the Neptune, Ralph Miller had a pigeon loft where he raised and raced several breeds of pigeons.

Between the Neptune and Dolphin was Mrs. J. F. Parker's "Free Museum" where you could buy pressed sea moss, souvenirs, and curios. Mrs. Parker hunted for sea moss at low tide, floated her specimens in a tin, and then mounted them on cards. She also wove sea moss into shapes such as hearts and crosses, or framed them. Visitors kept collections of sea moss in scrapbooks. Mrs. Parker also carried shells such as abalone, clams, and sand dollars.

"The glorious breakers as they swept landward were full of the sun's light, which as the overtopping crests broke into foam, made the fine spray more like diamond dust than water".
~ *Santa Cruz Daily Surf*, May 22, 1889

Leibbrandts and Millers Join Forces

In 1889, the Miller Brothers and the Leibbrandt Brothers decided to join forces and unite their bathing establishments under one roof. The two companies formed a partnership. They established one schedule of prices for baths: 25 cents for the single bath (hot or surf), or five tickets for one dollar. The combination benefited both the proprietors and the customers, being more efficient and entitling guests to more amenities.

They made numerous improvements to both bathhouses, creating hundreds of dressing rooms all furnished in redwood and fine wallpaper. New amenities included a saloon, a photography gallery, private offices, broad porches with views of the bay, and a candy store. The partners updated their plunge baths every year with the latest technology, and with their small army of swimming instructors and staff, created a thriving resort that catered to their customers' every need.

Grand Hotels

Built in 1894, the Vue de L'Eau was constructed as part of the trolley line promotion by J.P. Smith, a wealthy New York and Paris businessman, and was located on the corner of Garfield (Woodrow) and West Cliff Drive, near Pelton. Vue de L'Eau was planned as a family resort with a main floor lounge and restaurant and a second floor ballroom. Behind the building was a football field, a racetrack, and a baseball diamond that was used before the sport was moved to Dolphin Park. The resort later suffered hard times and was eventually demolished for a real estate subdivision.

The Pacific Ocean House was another popular hotel. It was considered one of the state's top seven coastal resorts in the 1890s, the others being the Piedmont, Cliff House,

"The softness of the wind, and the genial warmth of the sun were in striking contrast with the snow and sleet and cold which are now inflicting their rigors upon the unfortunate denizens of the Eastern and Middle States. Truly our Santa Cruz is the veritable Eden of the modern world." ~ A Santa Cruz Day, *Santa Cruz Daily Surf*, November 15, 1890

10 Capitola, Del Monte, Manhattan Beach, and Coronado. The Pacific Ocean House had rambling and sprawling Victorian grounds, and a world-famous botanical garden. The building was constructed on Beach Hill in the 1870s by S.A. Hall, a former ship builder who also built the Soquel Congregational Church. Hall originally named it the Ocean View House. The first building was bounded by Beach Street, Second Street, Main Street, and Drift Way. In 1882 it was renamed Douglas House when a Chicago artist bought it and added a third story, expanding it to 32 rooms. He also filled it with a large collection of California paintings. He sold the hotel in 1886 to D.K. Abeel who leased it to John T. Sullivan. The hotel was losing money so it was moved back toward Second Street and remodeled.

Plate 23 ~ Long white building in front of the sand says "no sharks here," "lodging," "baths." The shark claim came about after Father Hudson, a Catholic pastor from Gilroy, was brought from the water bleeding with his leg lacerated. The story appeared in the newspaper as a shark attack and set off a wave of panic among swimmers. [Courtesy of the Harold J. van Gorder Collection]

Plate 24 ~ Vue de L'Eau luxury family resort didn't do well. [Courtesy of the Harold J. van Gorder Collection]

Plate 25 ~ Sea Beach Hotel about 1900 with new wing in the distance. [Courtesy of the Harold van Gorder collection]

The new incarnation was renamed the Sea Beach Hotel. It featured tennis and croquet in the back. Abeel purchased the old Powder works warehouse at Main and Second streets and used the bricks and 50,000 feet of lumber to construct a new hotel wing. He hired architect G.W. Page to emulate the famed Coronado Hotel. Page

Plate 26 ~ The Sea Beach Hotel. The hotel was later destroyed by fire on June 12, 1912. This is the Main Street view from Second Street. [Courtesy of the Harold J. van Gorder Collection]

installed redwood floors, elevators, and 170 guest rooms each having a bedroom, parlor, bathroom, fireplace, electric lights, and telephone. The main entrance was on the second floor and led into an immense dining hall and porch overlooking the bay. The kitchen was carved into the hillside, and a miniature railway shuttled supplies to the dining room. Chefs came from the Hotel Del Monte and Chicago's Palmer House, serving nine-course meals on special occasions.

Plate 27 ~ Regatta ships outside of Sea Beach Hotel. [Courtesy of the Harold J. van Gorder Collection]

Santa Cruzan Rudolph Ulrich was superintendent of landscape design for the 1893 Chicago World's Fair, and he contracted with Sullivan to use plantings from his gardens to create a world-class botanical garden. John Thorp, chief of the fair's floral department, was amazed at the varieties he saw at the hotel and brought in a New York seed company to catalog 40 rose varieties, including the Sea Beach Beauty, Pride of Santa Cruz, and Loma Prieta. Seeds from these roses were sold worldwide.

A "Paris Opera" staircase led from the lobby to a ballroom. Dance lessons were offered during the day, and on summer evenings George W. Parkman's orchestra played for guests. Many early Santa Cruz residents learned to dance at the Sea Beach. The hotel hosted conventions, exhibits, shows, and high school dances. Two U.S. Presidents, Harrison and Roosevelt, stayed there. They also hosted officers of the Atlantic Fleet, Thomas Edison's son, Andrew Carnegie, William Randolph Hearst, Nob Hill socialites, and leading artists and writers of the day.

Plate 28 ~ Beach area in 1890s. [Courtesy of The Museum of Art & History@The McPherson Center, Santa Cruz, California]

Water Carnival

When a fire gutted downtown Santa Cruz in 1894, the city decided to rebuild its civic center in Renaissance styles and bill Santa Cruz as the "Florence of the West." James Philip Smith was a local wealthy businessman who had recently converted the Kittredge Hotel on Beach Hill into his private home. Smith's wife called it the Sunshine Villa. He created a lagoon on the San Lorenzo River and hosted the first weeklong Santa Cruz Venetian Water Carnival in 1895. The idea was an extension of the floral fairs of the state fair pavilion. A huge floral pavilion was constructed for costume balls and the coronation of the first carnival queen, Anita Gonzales, Smith's stepdaughter. The brand new all-steel ships of the Pacific Fleet were anchored offshore, seen by many for first time. The Fleet staged a mock battle, then were met at the beach by Queen Anita and pelted with flowers. The Queen led a floral parade down Pacific Avenue. Later a rose regatta of decorated boats, music, and stage entertainment was paraded down the river. The "Aquatic

Sports of the Water Olympics" was held, one year before the first modern Olympics, and featured swimming, diving, canoeing, and yachting. A velodrome on West Cliff Drive hosted a cycling event. The penultimate day was "Hi Jinks Day" when Santa Cruzans dressed up in masquerade and burlesque. Another parade was held with a fat man in a dress crowned the hobo queen, who then floated down the river on a garbage barge and was hoisted by tack and rope to the throne. When Venice, California opened in 1904, their superior development of the Venetian theme eclipsed Santa Cruz, and the water carnivals ended until 1912.

Fabulous Fred

Fred W. Swanton was the father of the Boardwalk. He was a well-known Santa Cruz promoter and entrepreneur, and later a three-term mayor of Santa Cruz.

Swanton was born to Mr. and Mrs. A.P. Swanton on April 11, 1862 in New York. As a young boy he visited Coney Island, an experience that left in indelible impression on him. He moved with his parents to Santa Cruz in 1868, attended Santa Cruz public schools and later graduated from Heald's Business School in San Francisco in 1881. The same year he accepted a position as bookkeeper with the Madera Flume and Trading Company in the Sierra Nevada mountains. He married Emma Stanley P. Hall in 1884.

Plate 29 ~ Art & History@The McPherson Center, Santa Cruz, California]

Plate 30 ~ Swanton House hotel in downtown Santa Cruz. The Swanton House was located on the corner of Water Street and Front Street, the site of present-day Santa Cruz Post Office. They also operated the Bonner Stables next door. [Courtesy of the Harold J. van Gorder Collection]

Swanton had a diverse and rich career in many areas. Among his many projects were establishing a fish hatchery in Brookdale and building an electric railway connecting Capitola and Santa Cruz. Swanton fielded local professional baseball teams, played a bit part in the infant California movie industry, took part in the Alaskan gold rush at the turn of the century, developed oil fields in Bakersfield, and later owned a chrome mine in the Sierra Nevada mountains.

Swanton had his share of failures, too. In 1883 he built a hotel, Swanton House, but it was destroyed in a fire May 30, 1887 that started in nearby Hong Lee's Wash House. Later hopes for a large subdivision at the western end of Santa Cruz didn't materialize, but he deeded most the land and beach for Natural Bridges State Park.

Swanton eventually went bankrupt in 1930, his $100 salary as mayor not enough to cover his $57,000 in personal debts. He died in September 1940 at the age of 78.

Swanton's early role in the utility industry gave him contacts and capital for his projects. In 1890 he started the Santa Cruz Electric Light and Power Company with partner Dr. H.H. Clark. Six years later they merged with Big Creek Power Company above Davenport. Swanton sold his rights to John Martin in 1906. The power companies quickly ran lines to Santa Cruz, effectively ending horse-drawn car transportation and permitting the first electric lighting.

Plate 31 ~ Swanton's Palace of Pharmacy advertisement. Probably about 1900. [Courtesy of The Museum of Art & History@The McPherson Center, Santa Cruz, California]

Plate 32 ~ Abel Arellanes, July 1897 Santa Cruz baseball player. [Courtesy of the Harold J. van Gorder Collection]

Swanton and his partners built the first hydroelectric plant west of Chicago, located in the Santa Cruz Mountains. Swanton also developed the community's electric streetcar system, the Santa Cruz Electric Railway, which ran streetcars between the beach and the town.

In 1887 Swanton went into the billboard business, eventually selling the business to George Birkenseer. That same year Swanton and William Ellery went into show business at the Knight Opera House producing a continuing program of professional shows. Swanton remained intrigued by show business and over the years continually tried to attract movie producers to film in the area for the publicity value to Santa Cruz.

His fascination with show business continued in 1903 when Swanton started The New Santa Cruz Entertainment Fund, providing 80 consecutive days and nights of entertainment (mostly bands) during the summer. Local citizens were encouraged to donate to the fund as a public service.

Plate 33 ~ Swanton's Big Creek Power Company building, Big Creek, California. Originally built in 1892 to develop power for the streetcar line to Vue de l'Eau. Water was delivered by a flume. [Courtesy of the Harold J. van Gorder Collection]

The concept of making Santa Cruz the "Atlantic City of the West," patterned after the Coney Island of Swanton's youth, began to dominate his thinking. In 1906, he sold his interest in his three power companies plus the Union Traction (train and trolley) Company to S. Waldo Coleman to generate capital and free his time. Martin continued to provide overall management for the companies until 1913 when Coleman took over and renamed it the Coast Counties Gas and Electric Company.

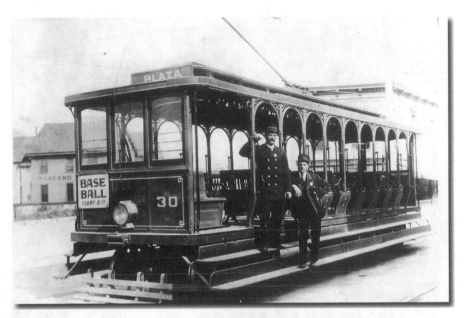

Plate 34 ~ Electric trolley going to the Dolphin Baseball Park. These trolleys were called Open Bench Summer Cars. The conductors are posing at the Plaza, ready to return to the Casino via Pacific Avenue. [Courtesy of the Harold J. van Gorder Collection]

Plate 35 ~ Knight's Opera House 1877-1892. Located on Park Street (now lower Union) between Chestnut Avenue and Vine Street, across from the old Santa Cruz railroad depot. It was dismantled in 1921. [Courtesy of the Harold J. van Gorder Collection]

Plate 36 ~ Opera House stage. [Courtesy of the Harold J. van Gorder Collection]

Plate 37 ~ Fred and wife Emma Swanton. Taken April 23, 1931 at the old Capitola Airport during a visit by Walter Hinton, an early trans-Atlantic flyer. [Courtesy of the Harold J. van Gorder Collection]

The Boardwalk Concept Forms

By 1903, approximately 100,000 visitors were coming to Santa Cruz every year to visit the beach, baths, and local attractions. There had been many discussions among city businessmen about forming a high quality beachside attraction to encourage more tourism. Locally the Hihns had done extremely well developing Capitola and had been able to fund all growth out of operating profits. Trips to other amusement areas confirmed that amusements brought lots of new visitors and resulting income to those communities.

With the announcement of an upcoming visit by President Theodore Roosevelt, Santa Cruz became concerned with improvement of its beach facilities. Building an esplanade was proposed as a step towards making the Santa Cruz beach more attractive to visitors. The City granted a franchise to Swanton's Santa Cruz-Capitola Railroad Company to construct and operate an electric railway along the beach. As part of the contract, the railway agreed to pay two-thirds of the total cost of building and constructing a new esplanade along the beach.[1]

Plate 38 ~ Pre-Casino picture. Notice how the entrance curved around the building onto the promenade deck. Electric trolley cars have arrived. [Courtesy of the Harold J. van Gorder Collection]

The City made use of two other subsidies to complete the construction of the esplanade. A civic women's organization, The Improvement Society, sponsored a fund-raising drive in conjunction with the Sea Beach Hotel and the mayor asked for some of those funds to be used in partial payment for building the esplanade.

In addition, James D. Phelan donated seats to the city to be used on the esplanade for the accommodations of the public. As a final step to improve the beach-front environment, the city council approved an ordinance which prohibited the 'hawking, vending, or selling of goods, wares, merchandise… on the ocean beach within the corporate limits of the City of Santa Cruz."[2]

Encouraged by successes in Atlantic City, Coronado, Long Beach, and Catalina, and by the success of the new Santa Cruz project, Swanton decided to launch a formal project to build what would ultimately be known as the Boardwalk. An estimated one million people lived within a day's travel of Santa Cruz so the potential was huge.

Swanton's original thought was to form a tent city adjacent to the beach, taking down private barbed wire fences that hindered beach access, getting Southern Pacific to grant leases to land they owned at the beach, and scheduling trains to Santa Cruz from surrounding areas. Southern Pacific would use its advertising power to attract visitors.

The "bathing beach" was considered the key to the area, specifically the strip of land north of the ocean from the site of the Neptune bath house to the mouth of the San Lorenzo River. The nearby hotels, boarding houses, and bathhouses would greatly benefit along with any local businesses in the surrounding area.

A *Santa Cruz Daily Surf* editorial in October 1903 encouraging the development project noted that the current primitive beach facilities and lack of aesthetic beauty disappointed first-time visitors. They used the example of a noted photographer who had been brought in to provide a scenic picture of the beach for advertising purposes, but in the end the project was cancelled because the area did not show well.

Southern Pacific was seen as the key power that Santa Cruz had to convince. Swanton moved cautiously because the railroad industry in other cities had completely owned and dominated the amusement areas leaving local business people without a voice. Santa Cruz wanted at least an equal partnership from the beginning.

Initial local capital was needed to provide operating funds, but equally important was a way to show local community support. On October 2, 1903 Swanton briefed citizens in the local courthouse about the proposed project to develop the area. Representatives from the railroads, local builders, and prominent businessmen were present. Swanton helped sell the concept by showing on paper that stock ownership should provide a return of 20-25 percent, considerably higher than the 4-6 percent common return on other investments at the time. His sales pitch was that it was a good investment, plus it gave people a voice in what happened to the area and helped the entire city. He displayed stylized renderings of a proposed casino and the tent and cottage city. The crowd was enthusiastic.

Swanton estimated that an initial $50,000 would be needed to start work. Obviously, more would be needed to bring the area up to full potential, but the first successful steps were vital. At the meeting, several people stepped forward immediately pledging funds and many others joined in shortly afterwards. Indicative of the local expansive mood, Judge Logan, proprietor of the Brookdale Lodge, said he would donate three lots at the beach and $500, expecting no return but doing it as a good citizen.

Ultimately, the unprecedented promotional efforts of Swanton created a tourist boom with the development of new attractions at the city beach. Throughout the final years of the 19th century, the seaside town attempted to compete with Monterey for elite visitors. But the new Casino, Plunge, and tent cabins that Swanton built set the stage for a trade that emphasized the volume of visitors over their economic status. It was a wildly successful strategy. Swanton didn't invent tourism, but he became so identified with the local industry that some people dubbed the city "Swanta Cruz."

The Boardwalk Takes Form

At age 40 Swanton was fully committed to the Boardwalk project. On October 29, 1903 he officially formed the Santa Cruz Beach, Cottage, and Tent City Corporation (SCBC&TC), known as the Santa Cruz Beach Company by locals, with an initial stock offering of 452 shares at a par value of $25 per share, generating an initial working capital of $113,025. The goal was to sell 40,000 shares and raise one million dollars. Henry Willey was President, Fred Swanton Director-General, and H.E. Irish, Secretary. F.R. Walti, George Staffler, H.F. Kron, and Thomas W. Kelly were the other incorporators. Each original incorporator purchased $4,000 of the $25 stock except Kron and Swanton who each purchased 10 shares. The first temporary headquarters were in the offices of future Boardwalk architect Edward L. Van Cleeck.

There was concern about the ability to raise sufficient funds and Swanton wrestled with Southern Pacific management who was essential to lease needed land in the area. They demanded a show of more participation to demonstrate real commitment. Many people, including those living out of the area, stated that they really didn't expect financial gains or even normally purchased stock, but in this case they were willing to subscribe for the "kindly feeling and good will they have towards Santa Cruz."[3] A carefully managed publicity campaign made it popular to support the effort by subscribing to the stock and literally hundreds of people eventually purchased an estimated 60,000 shares.

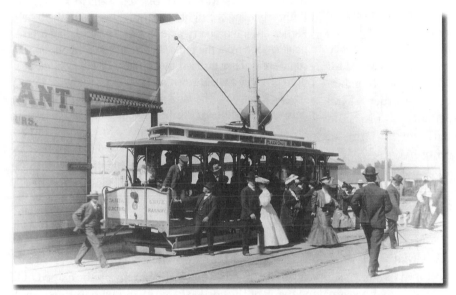

Plate 39 ~ Electric trolley car in the beach area. [Courtesy of the Harold J. van Gorder Collection]

Swanton and Irish visited influential people throughout California trying to raise funds and eventually $1.5 million was gathered by issuing stock, all of which was used to build the facilities and associated equipment. With the increasing number of subscriptions, including the original incorporators purchasing more stock, the mood shifted from "what if" to "we can do this" and in November requests for construction bids were published in the local Santa Cruz papers.

Swanton purchased the Miller and Leibbrandt baths for $28,000 in stock along with some additional land. The Miller property consisted of the old Neptune bathhouse and property across the railroad tracks occupied by the Miller aviary. The Leibbrandt bathhouse and concessions on the beach were also acquired. The Mills building (which housed the seashell store, restaurant, and other concessions) was razed and moved across the track away from the beach. It later became the Tent City Restaurant. The original Neptune was moved across the railroad tracks to the foot of Cliff Street, while the newer plunge baths became part of the casino. Both structures burned in the fire of June 22, 1906.

In 1904, after considerable lobbying, the City of Santa Cruz granted the SCBC&TC permission to construct the first commercial buildings on the beach. In April the Beach Company also asked for an exclusive franchise "to construct and maintain a pier and wharf for a term of twenty-five years."[4] The City Council vote was tied over the issue of who should get the revenue generated by the pier, but newly

BEACH OWNERSHIP

The argument over who rightfully owned the beachfront went through several rounds. In 1889, Judge McCann of the Superior Court of Santa Cruz County ruled in the City of Santa Cruz vs. Mrs. H.M. Blackburn and Mrs. Margaret Roth, regarding the rights of private persons to the beach. Parties owning property adjacent to the beach had been hauling sand from the public beach and erected buildings in some areas. They claimed ownership of the beach under a deed given by the old town of Santa Cruz to the California Powder Company. The land parcel included the area between the Southern Pacific Railroad, the low tide waters of the Monterey Bay, the San Lorenzo River, and the wharf of the rail company. Judge McCann ruled that the beach belonged to the City of Santa Cruz and its residents, because the area had been used continually by the public for recreation and exercise, to an even greater extent than the streets, squares, or public places in town. The [ownership dispute] continued until the 1930s.

elected Mayor David C. Clark broke the tie and the franchise was granted to Swanton. His strong support of Clark's election campaign no doubt helped. This debate about who was paying many of the costs (the city) and who was getting the revenue (the Beach Company) continues even until today.

The Neptune Casino

On June 14, 1904, now a 42 year-old millionaire, Swanton built and opened the Neptune Casino, including a city liquor license, at a cost of $204,000. Edward L. Van Cleeck was the original architect. The Casino was named after the successful nearby Neptune baths. Architecture of the first casino was based on the famous Alhambra in Spain, complete with 19 onion domes, a café, a ballroom, roof gardens, and arches painted in bright colors. Each side of the building had a separate unique façade.

The Casino was located across from Main Street and had 245 feet of beachfront property. A 35-foot-wide arcade faced the beach and extended the entire length of the building. Visitors liked to sit on the railing facing the beach and watch people enjoying the beach. An upstairs grill and dining room seating 500 could be opened into a larger room with a capacity of 4,000 people. A second floor elliptical-shaped theater seating 2,500 would be used for theatrical or grand opera productions and included nine dressing rooms and a 35-foot stage opening. There were 12 boxes, six above and six below, for high society. Twenty-two rooms on the second floor could also be used for meetings. A third floor rotunda had an observatory that allowed views far out into the ocean.

Plate 40 ~ Neptune Casino in about 1905. People still rode horses on the beach until the Boardwalk management talked the city into banning them. Sign towards the right side of the lower building says "oriental fish pond". [Courtesy of Covello and Covello Collection]

The lower floor contained 16 rooms including a barbershop and hair dressing parlor, and an ice cream and candy shop. A lighted beach bandstand on the sand hosted concerts and there were hundreds of lounging chairs on the porches. Adjoining the pavilion were the public baths with a 140 x 70-foot pool with warm and cold salt water, sun parlors, and a laundry. About 200 workmen were engaged in the construction of the casino.

Plate 41 ~ Workers building the first casino (1904). [Courtesy of The Museum of Art & History at The McPherson Center, Santa Cruz, California]

Plate 42 ~ Casino "Rotunda" dining room. [Courtesy of California Santa Cruz Special Collections Library]

Pleasure Pier

A 400-foot pier was built over the intake pipes that took in water for the Plunge to the south of the main city wharves and connecting with the wooden boardwalk. It became known as the "Pleasure Pier" or later the "Electric Pier" because it was rimmed by electric lights.

The Pleasure Pier cost $1,000 to build, with the new Beach Company supplying the materials. An iron railing ran the whole length with iron posts for electric lights. In June 1904, bright vermilion-hue seats were placed along the sides of the pier. On the seaward side it ended in a 20 x 62-foot T-shaped area. Springboards, slides, and a trapeze were available for amusement.

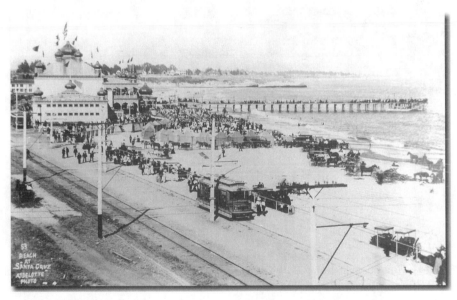

Plate 43 ~ Electric trolley #11, old Casino, at Pleasure Pier before extension. You could ride anywhere in Santa Cruz for 5¢. Summer of 1905. [Courtesy of the Harold J. van Gorder Collection]

A neoclassical lighthouse at the end of the pier was the ticket booth for boat rides. In October 1904 Swanton told the *Santa Cruz Daily Surf* of eventual plans to lengthen the pier so more people could use it.

Tent City

To ensure that visitors had a place to stay, close to his businesses, Swanton built a Tent City on the former Dolphin baseball field with over 220 (later 300) red and white striped tent "cottages" built over wooden frames with a wooden floor, each with electric lighting and water. Rent was from $3.50 to $10.00 per week.[5]

Plate 44 ~ Tent city from the top of the Casino building. Probably 1905. [Courtesy of University of California Santa Cruz Special Collections Library]

These provided low-cost alternatives to the more expensive neighboring rooming houses and luxury hotels like the Sea Beach Hotel, and immediately became popular with tourists. The Cotton Brothers provided a suction dredging machine that inexpensively and easily transferred sand into the Tent City area to provide a clean, level surface. Iron posts were placed around the tent area to keep horses out and one dirt road entrance on what is today's Cliff Street was created for horse teams to use. In 1905 some of the tents were removed and a large "office" tent was put in their place, which was also used for social events and included a piano, evening card parties, and receptions. The corporation eventually paid

$32,000 for the Mills, Miller, and Leibbrandt properties where the Tent City resided. Mr. Lynn Austin was Manager of Tent City, assisted by Mrs. Hagan and eight female assistants. Sheets, pillowcases, blankets, and towels initially cost $3,000 and were provided by Samuel Leask of the Seaside Store, T.W. Kelly of the Racket, and A.C. Snyder.

8403. THE TENT CITY, SANTA CRUZ, CALIF.

Plate 45 ~ Red and white striped Tent City and the first Casino. From a color postcard. [Courtesy of the Harold J. van Gorder Collection]

Tent City became very popular and many prominent visitors reserved tents or suites of tents for the entire summer season.

Power House

The Beach Company directors wanted thousands of lights at the Boardwalk and knew that electricity was becoming a major expense. After failing to reach agreement with the local light company they decided to build their own power-house to primarily serve the Boardwalk area. Excess power would be sold to downtown businesses (many of them owned by the Company directors). The 97 x 100-foot Coast Counties Power building was started in the same architectural style as the Casino. It was in operation by June with the equivalent of 4,000 horsepower of electrical generating capacity. The building was located north and east of the Casino, across the rail tracks.

First Opening

The official opening of the Neptune Casino was held June 11, 1904. The Third Artillery Band opened the season and the Grand Promenade Concert and Ball commenced at 8 p.m. Admission to the Casino and Ball were free. Swanton ran electric lights over the river and outlined all of the buildings, then lit up the night sky with a fireworks display. The California Fireworks Company provided a pyrotechnics show. All of the tents were lit and open to visitors for inspection. The new beauty parlor opened, owned by Dr. Schley, and Mr. Riley ran the candy department. A new soda fountain, weighing 2,000 pounds, dispensed refreshments and there was a dumb waiter so they could service both floors.

Swanton held a reception and hundreds of people stopped by to congratulate him on the success of his venture. Mayor Clark formally dedicated the Casino in an opening address. Representatives from the rail lines also spoke on the potential of Santa Cruz, and how the Casino would be a lodestone that would draw thousands of visitors every year. The Armand Putz band played on the bandstand. At 10:30 p.m. the crowds dedicated the ballroom and did the two-step and waltz until midnight.

Lounging on the beach was permitted for "properly attired folks" but many locals and visitors took advantage of the hot baths and warm indoor salt water Plunge facilities. Mrs. Molitor was in charge of the hot salt water baths.

An impromptu celebration was held one night after the initial Boardwalk opening. Guests toured Tent City and then had a gourmet dinner prepared by Chef Maurice Catz in the new Neptune Grill in the Casino building. Mayor Clark led a series of speeches praising the new endeavor, noting how much it benefited the city in general. "Swanton put emphasis upon the liberality of the merchants and businessmen – and the lack of it in property owners." [6]

A week after the opening, one of the large elevated water tanks east of the hot baths came down after an accidentally removed plug allowed water to flow out, eventually undermining the tank platform. It was quickly replaced. The large number of people in the area made safety an increasing concern so J.H. Wallace, Chief Engineer of the Southern Pacific Railroad, agreed to permanently reduce the speed of trains moving through the Boardwalk area.

Plate 46 ~ The Bathing Pavilion, Santa Cruz. On the Road of a Thousand Wonders." From a color postcard. [Courtesy of the Harold van Gorder Collection]

The SCBC&TC Corporation issued a public financial statement in September 1904 giving a summary of operating funds since the corporation's beginnings in the fall of 1903. This does not include the initial capital expenditures:

Dept	Disbursements	Receipts	Balance
Bar	$9,848.99	$15,896.15	$ 6,047.16
Plunge	1,408.00	4,648.90	3,240.90
Surf	791.35	3,209.75	2,418.40
Tent City	1,911.25	3,926.20	2,041.95
Hot Baths	527.75	1,680.90	1,053.15
Casino	4,221.64	5,026.52	804.88
Pier	135.70	384.60	248.90
Laundry	825.34	876.34	51.00
Rest. Grill & Kitchen	3,186.13	11,817.84	(1,368.29)
TOTAL	$32,856.15	$47,367.20	$14,511.05

Based on the statement, the bar generated the most revenue, followed by the Plunge, but the food services lost money. It was assumed that the Plunge and baths were the real profit centers so a revised statement was issued showing just "the 1904 season."

	Gain	Loss
Plunge Baths	$ 8,121.06	
Bar	6,745.31	
Surf Bathing	2,564.98	
Tent City	2,036.01	
Casino, Ball Room, Attractions	1,588.12	
Hot Baths	1,087.97	
Pier account	232.20	
Laundry	132.22	
Rest. Grill & Kitchen		1,971.82
TOTAL	$ 17,567.87	$1,971.82
TOTAL GAIN	$15,596.05	

In its first year the Boardwalk was profitable and very popular both with locals and visitors.

1905 Season

After the first highly successful season ended, Swanton immediately began plans for expansion.

The Pleasure Pier was extended 100 feet that fall and a new 40 x 80-foot concession pavilion was built. The approach to the Pleasure Pier was also expanded. Swanton built a wooden boardwalk from the end of the bathhouse to the mouth of the river, enlarged the restaurant, and had a new glass front constructed at the front of the Casino to allow for better ocean views. Construction began on a 60 x 22-foot aquarium in front of the baths. The barbershop was enlarged to five chairs, and a suit store was removed; in its place a large horseshoe-shaped counter for serving ice cream and sodas was installed. The Tent City restaurant, run by P. Carstulovich and M. Coserich, was remodeled with a glass front at the end facing the Casino.

Swanton obtained the rights to "ice cream cornucopias" for the county, which allowed for the eating of ice cream without "soiling the dainty gloves." Concessions in 1905 included glass blowing, box ball, pond fishing, a shooting gallery, a raffle wheel, fairy floss candy, and the fairy letter writer. Swanton planned to add a bowling alley and a shooting gallery.

1905 SEASON. George Moss was appointed manager of the Casino Bar, Mrs. L. Hagen housekeeper of Tent City, Hugh Metzler cashier, "Bobby" Gordell, assistant, and Perry Gross of Fresno was in charge of the ballroom. Billy Gross was in charge of entertainment; W.J. Carpenter ran the soda fountain. Madame Zara was the palmist, J.T. McKean ran the photo tintype gallery, and the penny arcade was leased to Mr. Hawes.

Plate 47 ~ Pleasure Pier improvements – date unknown, but after the fire. [Courtesy of the Covello and Covello Collection]

Swanton proposed to the City of Santa Cruz and Capitola Railroad that they jointly purchase the existing Southern Pacific Railroad bridge across the San Lorenzo River and move it slightly north so that it would connect directly with the Boardwalk. He envisioned use by both pedestrians and trains, with Capitola only 15 minutes away by train.

That same year a boat was commissioned to make two daily trips to Monterey for tourists during the summer and to take fishing parties to the Laguna reefs north of Santa Cruz.

Private tents were prohibited on the beach so as "not to block the view" although some saw this as a way to prevent "undesirables" from using the beach. The Casino management installed a 350-foot-long, 24-foot-wide awning to create a shady area for visitors watching the activities on the beach. The City agreed to clean the beach every morning and supply additional police presence.

Tent City officially opened pre-season on May 20 and the bands began playing on June 3. The Butchers and Grocers from San Jose and the Italian Benevolent Society were booked as early conventions. The auditorium featured vaudeville acts and moving pictures. Nightly stereopticon presentations were given advertising local Santa Cruz attractions.

Automobiles began to appear in 1905, although at a $900 cost most people still preferred horses and buggies.

Plate 48 ~ Casino in the foreground, hot air balloon in the distance. Probably late 1910s. [Courtesy of University of California Santa Cruz Special Collections Library]

New to the Boardwalk that summer was the "Captive Balloon." It was 65 feet in diameter, held 10,000 cubic feet of hot air, and rose to about 3,000 feet on a good day. The balloon was anchored at the pier alongside a fire pit that generated the hot air. Harold van Gorder remembers, *"A fully inflated balloon carried a man on a trapeze seat. At the proper height, where it could be observed along the entire waterfront, he pulled a ripcord and floated earthward in a parachute. It was an exciting crowd pleaser."*[7]

A brand new "Flying Bird" was also a hit. From the balloon, a man climbed aboard a glider machine and, cut loose from the balloon, and could glide for up to 30 minutes in the area.

World champion roller skater Harley Davidson opened a new rink in March 1906. The roller skating rink had a brass band that supplied the music. It was very popular and later survived the big fire.

"They had a skating rink. I can remember we would go down there — we were suppose to go to church on Sunday nights, instead we'd go down to the skating rink. And then at nine o'clock, we'd have to run like the devil to get back home so our folks thought we'd been in church."[8]

Things seemed grand at the end of the second season and Swanton's team was optimistic about the future.

Plate 49 ~ Hot air balloon inflating for ascension. Crowd surrounds beach fire pit where heat for the balloon was generated. 1912. [Courtesy of the Harold J. van Gorder Collection]

Fire! Tragedy Strikes

Tragedy struck on June 22, 1906. An early morning fire from a stove in the upstairs ballroom kitchen destroyed the Neptune Casino, the Miller and Leibbrandt Plunge Baths, the bandstand, plus the Tent City Restaurant and the Dabelich Restaurant across the street.

Plate 50 ~ Boardwalk fire in June 1906, only two years after the Dolphin Casino first opened. [Courtesy of the Covello and Covello Collection]

A Tent City employee first noticed the blaze and turned in the alarm at 5:00 a.m. that Friday morning. A night watchman had moved through the area 20 minutes earlier and hadn't noticed any problems. Later, Boardwalk Publicity Director and historian Skip Littlefield reported that: *"The water pressure was down in the city mains and they couldn't fight it and it went up in smoke, the whole thing right to the ground... One theory was crossed electric wires resulting in some manner from the manipulations of carpenters who had been working in the attic and on the roof, cutting in ventilators. These holes in the roof caused a draft that fanned the fire."*

The fire burned for an hour and a half fanned by northwest winds before finally burning itself out. There was only $70,000 insurance on the complex and many people lost money as a result, especially the independent vendors. Coming only two months after the great San Francisco earthquake, things at first seemed bleak, especially for San Franciscans who had come to Santa Cruz after the earthquake to recover. Luckily, most of the foundation piles were not damaged, making future work easier, and the concrete tank of the Plunge survived. Also left were the Pleasure Pier, Tent City, the powerhouse, merry-go-round, and skating rink.

Plate 51 ~ Fire completely destroyed the new Casino building. It also destroyed several adjacent buildings because there wasn't sufficient water pressure to fight the fire. 1906. [Courtesy of the Covello and Covello Collection]

Most of the books and papers of the company were lost in the fire so many original records were gone forever. There was some discussion about suing the city for lack of water to fight the fire but company officials decided that alienating the city fathers was not in the long-term interests of the Boardwalk.

Rebuilding

A significant publicity campaign was launched immediately to assure people that the rest of the Boardwalk area remained open and ready for business. *Sentinel* headlines the next day announced *"Beach Buildings Will Rise, Phoenix-Like From Their Ashes."* [9]

Two days after the fire the Third Artillery Band from the Presidio of San Francisco gave its regular Sunday concert in a hastily rebuilt bandstand.

Plate 52 ~ Casino ruins still smoldering after the 1906 fire. Sea View Hotel is on the hill to the left. [Courtesy of University of California Santa Cruz Special Collections Library]

Swanton moved quickly and immediately constructed a large 60 x 150-foot circus tent to hold visitors for the summer events. In 1906 the Republican state convention was held in the tent and James N. Gillett was nominated for governor, eventually winning that race. The whole canvas tent was raised four feet with electric fans placed on poles to increase air circulation. Just outside the tent to the west Swanton provided three booths for Western Union, the Postal Telegraph, and Sunset Telephone Company. Fifteen tents were also built for newspaper reporters.

A few tents were moved from Tent City to the beach area to serve as changing rooms for visitors. *"After that bad fire, they put up tents on the beach proper. Therefore, for a small charge, you could be under a canopy. You could be exclusive. Fred was a promoter, there was no question about it. He had the push and he used to go bathing down there and he always wore a bathing suit from his neck all the way down to his ankles."* [10]

Plate 53 ~ 1906 rebuilding the Casino after the fire destroyed the building. Sea View Hotel is in the distance on the hill. [Courtesy of Covello and Covello Collection]

Other activities were set up in the merry-go-round building and at the skating rink. By July 4 a wooden dance floor had been placed over the Casino pilings. On July 6 the Plunge was opened, walled in by dressing rooms but with only the sky as a ceiling, although electric lights allowed night swimming. The ice cream stand, grill, shooting gallery, bar, Japanese bowling alley, barber shop, palmist, and candy stand were all relocated.

Swanton closed down the Santa Cruz Beach, Cottage & Tent City Corporation around November 1906 so that stockholders could avoid liability for previous debts that amounted to about $12.00 per share plus an additional $200,000. The reformed company was called the Santa Cruz Company. Previous stockholders were given equivalent amounts of preferred stock in the new company.

Famed architect William Henry Weeks of Watsonville was given broad authority to build an even better version of the Boardwalk and he based it on the Manufacturers' Pavilion at the 1894 San Francisco World's Fair.

Plate 54 ~ The "open air" pool that was temporarily opened after the first plunge building burned (1906). [Courtesy of University of California Santa Cruz Special Collections Library]

Swanton and the Beach Company were their own contractors for the rebuild, subcontracting portions of the work. Twenty-eight contractors had been invited to bid on the work but only two replies were received, one after the deadline, due to the shortage of building materials after the 1906 San Francisco earthquake, uncertainty about the economy, and the extremely tight deadline. Neither bid was opened and instead the company decided to do the work themselves.

F.R. Cummings was asked to be superintendent of construction. Michelangelo Garibaldi was commissioned to ornament the interior with Italian-inspired statues and an overall Rococo design. Rumors were that Garibaldi had a drinking problem and often had to be bailed out of jail so that he could complete his work. The company purchased additional land, including the remaining Leibbrandt property, the powerhouse, and the laundry building. Cottages replaced some of the tents. By October new foundations were being laid. Eventually $750,000 was

George H. Cardiff "claimed that the financial backing for the reconstruction of the Casino came from John Martin, a financier and manager of a utilities company which is now Pacific Gas and Electric, as it was really the utility company of San Francisco that built all of this here". This view finds agreement with Warren Littlefield, Seaside Company Publicity Manager, in a 1966 interview.

invested in the "new" Boardwalk, mostly money provided by Swanton's business partner, John Martin.

Plate 55 ~ Rebuilding the Casino and other buildings. January 19, 1907. [Courtesy of University of California Santa Cruz Special Collections Library]

The local press called the new buildings the "pride of the Pacific Coast," which continued with the Moorish and California Mission architectural influence. Some local critics called it the "ugly" casino, referring to semicircular, domed central pavilion with twin obelisks on the sides. Large domes dominated both ends of the Casino. Fire protection was a high priority and 2,000 sprinkler heads were installed along with a $3,000 asbestos curtain for the ballroom. A new shell-shaped bandstand was created. Three years later, two towers were erected on each side of the bandstand and seats behind the front row were elevated to make all the musicians visible. The band shell was later destroyed during winter storms.

The new grill space tried to create the feeling of Yosemite Valley. Papier maché covered the walls in natural colors and in the center of the space was a fountain with brook trout.

Because cash was tight, Swanton was forced to obtain additional outside financing to reduce the $33,000 he owed in debt to local merchants, and so that he could continue to work.

Plate 56 ~ Second Casino building under construction. Note the "loops" on the right which are the frames for the new plunge. March 3, 1907. [Courtesy of University of California Santa Cruz Special Collections Library]

Plate 57 ~ Rebuilding the boardwalk and plunge - 1906. [Courtesy of The Museum of Art & History@The McPherson Center, Santa Cruz, California]

Plate 58 ~ Construction crew rebuilding the Boardwalk 1906-7. [Courtesy of The Museum of Art & History@The McPherson Center, Santa Cruz, California]

Plate 59 ~ "Casino and Bandstand, Santa Cruz, California." Postcard [Courtesy of the Harold van Gorder Collection]

Plate 60 ~ 1907 saw the rebuilding of the Casino (as seen from Pleasure Pier). [Courtesy of Covello and Covello Collection]

Plate 61 ~ Rebuilt Casino from the water. [Courtesy of The Museum of Art & History@The McPherson Center, Santa Cruz, California]

Plate 62 ~ "Casino and Beach at Santa Cruz, California. On line of Southern Pacific." Official Southern Pacific Post Card. [Courtesy of the Harold van Gorder Collection]

Plate 63 ~ Crowds at the rebuilt Casino. Notice that the rented umbrellas are mostly wide stripes this year. [Courtesy of the Harold van Gorder Collection]

Cottage City

Tents were replaced with wooden cottages in 1906, an office to greet visitors was built on Beach Street, across and slightly north of the Casino, and the area was renamed "Cottage City." According to John Chace, "*The cottages were painted in such a way that they supposedly produced a rainbow effect when viewed from the hills.*"[11]

A 1910 visitors guide lists rates for the new Cottage City:

One person: $.75 to $1.00 per night; $5.00 to $7.00 per week

Two persons: $1.50 to $2.50 per night; $9.00 to $15.00 per week

Four persons: $2.50 to $3.50 per night; $15.00 to $28.00 per week

Eight persons: $40 per week

Plate 64 ~ Cottage City, bathing pavilion, and new Casino. Postcard, no date. [Courtesy of the Harold J. van Gorder Collection]

Plate 65 ~ The Cottage City office across from the Casino. Notice the dirt street. [Courtesy of The Museum of Art & History@The McPherson Center, Santa Cruz, California]

4032 An Avenue in Cottage City, Santa Cruz, Cal.

Plate 66 ~ Postcard looking towards the Casino. [Courtesy of the Harold J. van Gorder Collection]

Plate 67 ~ 1909 postcard showing Cottage City and the Casino and Plunge buildings. Dirt streets for the buggies. [Courtesy of the Harold J. van Gorder Collection]

The New Casino

The new Casino was a combined theater, dance pavilion, and dining room. It included six private dining rooms with Rupert Fritz in charge of catering facilities.

The Casino wasn't your normal gambling casino as the name suggests. Mrs. Howe, a 96-year-old resident of Santa Cruz whose husband was VP of the Seaside Company and mayor of Santa Cruz for several years, remembers the Casino quite clearly:

"Heavens no," exclaimed Mrs. Howe, *"it was never a gambling casino. The casino was a huge room filled with penny machines with little apertures through which people could peek to view illuminated scenery pictures."*[12]

Upstairs was a magnificent ballroom with windows overlooking Monterey Bay. According to the *Santa Cruz Sentinel*, the oval grand ballroom was 'an artist's dream of beauty.' The walls were decorated in cherry red with gold and murals of trees. The ceiling was buff, the stage was cream-colored with light, cool green highlights, and the chairs were cream and gold. The ballroom could seat about 2,500 guests, and the entertainment usually consisted of theatrical performances, magic shows, operas, and big band performances. The ballroom opened into an enormous rotunda grill with brilliantly lit crystal chandeliers, private dining rooms overlooking the bay, and a roof garden. The Grill Room restaurant included a complete butcher shop and imported Haviland china for banquets. "*In nearby areas private dining rooms were decorated according to various themes: Arts and Crafts, Japanese, German, English, and Dutch Delft Rooms. A replica of New York's Waldorf-Astoria bar formed a 40 x 40-foot parallelogram of highly polished, Honduran mahogany, with a serving frontage of 84 feet.*"[13]

Casino from Sea Beach Hotel, Santa Cruz, Cal.

Plate 68 ~ Casino viewed from Sea Beach Hotel. [Courtesy of the Harold J. van Gorder Collection]

At night every balcony, window, and archway was outlined and illuminated with electric bulbs.[14] An estimated 20,000 light bulbs outlined the main building and Plunge. Originally a stage dominated one end of the ballroom. On July 1, 1907, Nance O'Neil's "The Sorceress" opened the Casino Theatre. Famous names soon followed including: "*Wilton Lackaye in Hall Caine's "The Bondman"; Max Figman in "The Man on the Box" and Lew Dockstader and his great minstrel troupe of 70; Richard Jose, silvery tenor, with his renditions of "Dolly Gray" and "Silver Threads Among the Gold" still unforgettable. Also Pollard's Lilliputians in opera; "Coming Thru the Rye," a large musical, with young Sidney Toler prominent. He later rose to fame on the talking screen as Charlie Chan. The long list also includes: Kolb & Dill, May Robeson, Otis Skinner, Ferris Hartman, and Julian Eltinge, celebrated female impersonator.*" [15]

Plate 69 ~ Lower level, interior of the Casino building. Ice cream parlor on the left. White blouse figure in far right is selecting post cards at the J.W. Dickenson Curio Store (Harold van Gorder's sister worked there). Out of view in the lower right was Louis Sallee's Penny Arcade and the Lemos Studio where he painted scenes on diagonally cut redwood tree slabs. [Courtesy of the Harold J. van Gorder Collection]

Concessions

A penny arcade operated by Louis Sallee of San Francisco originally had machines featuring palmistry, astrology, horoscopes, the latest 1907 musical hits, mechanical singing birds, still picture machines, an automatic rifle and pistol range, five-cent slot machines, and a bathing girl picture machine. Sallee originally invested $12,000 in the machines and moved them to Sacramento every winter when the Casino was closed. He eventually sold his equipment to the Seaside Company in 1930.

The lower level contained a curio shop, barber shop, cigar store, newsstand, rooms for a hairdresser and a manicurist, an ice cream parlor, a Western Union office, ukulele store, a branch of the public library, a saloon, and an outdoor bandstand. The Sperry Flour Lady baked scones. A gated soda fountain sat in the middle of the penny arcade, surrounded by 150 oak-cased arcade machines. There was also the Boardwalk Theater that showed motion pictures.

Plate 70 ~ 1907 Boardwalk. Notice how the wooden "walk" extends towards the San Lorenzo River, with sand on both sides. [Courtesy of Covello and Covello Collection]

Plate 71 ~ 2nd floor of the Casino was a grand dance floor with balcony sitting. [Courtesy of University of California Santa Cruz Special Collections Library]

Plate 72 ~ Entrance to Casino. Postcard postmarked in 1913 "on the road of a thousand wonders." [Courtesy of the Harold J. van Gorder Collection]

Plate 73 ~ Crowd on Pleasure Pier. [Courtesy of the Harold van Gorder Collection]

Plate 74 ~ " Never a dull moment in Santa Cruz." Crows, Pleasure Pier, the Balboa ship, circa 1912. [Courtesy of the Harold van Gorder Collection]

Plate 75 ~ Casino at night. [Courtesy of the Harold van Gorder Collection]

"Another thing they used to have was Brashear's Candy Wagon. Well, I knew the little girl Roon, whose father pulled the taffy. In order to get business, he sold his taffy, and in each bag he put a letter of his name—Brashear--so if you ever got the name Brashear, you got a bag of candy. We'd hunt every bag in the sand to try and find a letter to complete the name Brashear. And, of course, you know darn well that they probably didn't put too many 'a's' in it."[16]

There were also sun parlors, a smoking room, 592 individual dressing rooms, an underground passageway to the beach, roller skating areas, a box ball court (an early form of bowling), and an archery range.

The Plunge

"...none left as great a heritage of lives touched with memories as did 'The Plunge,' as it was best known. Generations learned to swim there, and some learners later became beach lifeguards. In the kiddie or adult pools, with or without water wings, apprehensions were confronted, subsided, and victories claimed."[17]

Plate 76 ~ 1905 first Casino. [Covello and Covello Collection]

Plate 77 ~ 1908 rebuilt Casino. Contrast it with the picture immediately preceding this one to see the architectural changes that were made in the second Casino. [Courtesy of Covello and Covello Collection]

Plate 78 ~ "Catching Salmon in front of the Sea Beach Hotel, Santa Cruz, California. Geo. Webb, 400 Pacific Ave., Santa Cruz" (photographers). This is obviously a posed picture and has the Sea View Hotel in the background, but apparently not the Boardwalk so probably pre-1904. Not clear where it was taken, perhaps at the Webb studio. [Courtesy of the Harold J. van Gorder Collection]

Plate 79 ~ Same posed location as above. Back of the picture identifies Leland Stanford Jr. and wife. The famous founder of Stanford University died in 1893 so it is possibly them. [Courtesy of University of California Santa Cruz Special Collections Library]

Plate 80 ~ Early postcard of the train station. [Courtesy of the Harold J. van Gorder Collection]

Plate 81 ~ Roof of the new Plunge building 1906. [Courtesy of The Museum of Art & History@The McPherson Center, Santa Cruz, California]

Plate 82 ~ Plunge construction about 1907. [Courtesy of The Museum of Art & History@The McPherson Center, Santa Cruz, California]

The swimming Plunge, orNatatorium, was a 117 x 220-foot steel and glass building with 800 electric lights, ferns, and statues in the classical style. There were actually two pools: the larger 135 x 65-foot pool for men and a smaller pool in the same facility for ladies and children that was 30 x 60 feet.[18] Almost 400,000 gallons of warmed salt water was needed to fill the pools.

"A 16" pipe brought the sea water from under the Casino's Pleasure Pier to a Pacific Coast Gas and Electric sub-station across the street from the Plunge. The sub-station not only pumped the water from the ocean and into the Plunge but purified and heated the water to 84-85 degrees as well."[19]

"At its inception, the Plunge was decorated inside and out with replicas of Grecian statuary. It was fashioned by Michael Angelo Garibaldi, noted Italian sculptor. Scotsman John McLaren, father of Golden Gate Park, hung scores of tropical ferns and plants from the 50-foot girders. Five hundred incandescent globes provided pool illumination. They ringed the contour of the eight structural girders. Just in case the power failed, the balcony and lobby sported gaslight fixtures. One mile of neon tubular light replaced the gaslight and incandescent system in 1946. The pool was constructed

with two tanks that operated independently. The small pool (60 x 30 feet) was kept open around the seasons. Spring and summer operation was figured for the "large drink" which measured 135 feet by 65 feet. Capacity of the combined pools was 408,000 gallons. Depths ran from 2 ½ to 9 ½ feet. [20]

Plate 83 ~ Interior of the Plunge Bathing Pavilion. Postcard postmarked 1912. [Courtesy of the Harold J. van Gorder Collection]

The June 30, 1911 *Santa Cruz Daily Surf* quoted prices for bathing suits at The Arcade at 114 Pacific Avenue. "Men's or Boys' bathing suits 50c to $3.50; Ladies' Bathing Suits $1.75 to $5.00; Misses' Bathing Suits $1.50 to $2.50; Children's Bathing Suits 50c to $2.50; rubber caps 10c to $1.50; Bathing Shoes 25c and 35c." ~ Anonymous. *Bathing Suits or Accessories. Santa Cruz Daily Surf,* June 30, 1911, p unknown.

"From the balconies above the pool, people could observe all the swimmers (and later in the 1920s the water carnivals and high divers showing off their stunts from a 50-foot height). The Plunge facilities also offered swimming lessons, sun parlors, massage rooms, dressing rooms, and even a matron with a key to unlock the rooms. People could also rent towels and bathing suits, and parasols for sunbathing on the beach, and a tunnel ran from the beach to the showers so people could wash off the sand before using the Plunge." [21]

"When the Plunge was built here on the beach at Santa Cruz, it was quite a curiosity for spectators to come and watch anyone who could actually swim in deep water. The position of swimming instructor in those days was called the Professor of

Aquatic Natation. It was quite a lucrative operation in a period where you could buy a filet mignon steak smothered in mushrooms, for 25 cents. These swimming instructors during June, July, and August often made as much as a thousand dollars a month. To induce additional interest in swimming, Santa Cruz Beach Co. brought over from Australia Arthur Cavill. He is in the Encyclopedia Britannica. He was the originator of the Australian Crawl Stroke. He held a few world records at that time and his name was internationally known. He became the head swimming instructor here at Santa Cruz Beach. And as such he attracted a tremendous amount of attention and interest. The swimming pool attracted him. It was an outstanding swimming pool. Then in 1913 Santa Cruz Beach brought over probably the greatest swimmer of all time, the famous Duke Kahanamoku of Honolulu. It was standing room only whenever the Duke swam in the Plunge. Of course, the Duke..... [became] World Olympic Games Champion."[22]

Plate 84 ~ Drawing of the interior of the bathing pavilion. Postcard postmarked 1911. [Courtesy of the Harold J. van Gorder Collection]

The Amateur Athletic Union and official timers from the Olympic Club in San Francisco sponsored the event. Admission was 25 cents. Duke lowered his own world record in the 50-yard freestyle by two-fifths of a second, and he won a half-mile race in the bay.

"It was a weekly event, I think on Saturday night. It was the place to go. I remember, he [Littlefield] had some good talent in swimmers – underwater swimming, high divers, and he had his clowns – aquatic clowns. And then he had the fire dive.

"Bosco" was the high diver. The top of the Plunge, as you know, even today, is pretty high... and it wasn't high enough to be spectacular, so they opened up a hole in the roof, Don came down through the roof into nine or ten feet of water."[23]

Plate 85 ~ Don Patterson, known as "Bosco", slides from the roof of the Casino towards Pleasure Pier. [Courtesy of The Museum of Art & History@The McPherson Center, Santa Cruz, California]

"Bosco," or Don Patterson, was a member of the Santa Cruz Surfing Club and a lifeguard at Cowell Beach. He performed in the fire dive shows from 1927 to 1945. Wrapping himself first in protective clothing, he was doused with gasoline and set aflame, and then dove from a 45-foot high tower. Bosco performed the stunt an unbelievable 480 times, earning him the name, "Mighty Bosco." Ernie Dabade and Dido Scettrini were other divers who leaped from the highest points in the plunge to entertain the crowds.

"They had some really good clowns in that Aquacade. They were all local people and were all really good. They got up on the high board and one or two would mess around and one foot would slip and would hit the board with their whole body and bounce off into the water, off the high board. And they were all dressed up in old-fashioned bathing suits with stuff on, so they looked the part."

Plate 86 ~ Don Patterson and two boys performing at the Plunge. [Courtesy of The Museum of Art & History@The McPherson Center, Santa Cruz, California]

"One of the high points of the whole Aquacade was the race between one of the clowns and Duke Kahanamoku. The Duke would be up in a racing start and the other clown would be just lolling around in the water, in very silly poses and Skip Littlefield did a beautiful job announcing on this. He would build up the tension and get going and 'on your marks, get set,' then the gun would go off and Duke would hit the water with a beautiful racing dive and would be halfway across the water, and the clown would just be laying on his elbow in the gutter of the pool and lookin' around and all of a sudden he would start to go – and he'd go! The clown would go so fast that he'd lay a huge big wake of water in front of him and would pass him just at the last minute and reach the other side before Duke did. They had a rope lying on the bottom of the

pool and the clown would grab this and then a whole bunch of guys running down the side isle with a pulley. A body can really push a lot of water and there was just a huge wake of water in front of the clown and he would pretend like he was swimming all the time with little hand motions, above the water, dipping his fingers in once in a while." [24]

Plate 87 ~ Interior of the Plunge bathing pavilion. Postcard postmarked 1914. [Courtesy of the Harold J. van Gorder Collection]

Seaside Company directors removed the slides in 1919. The copper-plated human chutes were wearing out the seats of their rented bathing garments. Until 1920 the pools were drained and cleaned every night. In its heyday some 2,500 people could be provided with lockers and dressing room space at one time. Stocks of 4,000 towels and 2,000 suits were available. [25]

An aquarium building was built next to the Natatorium and included a pool for four alligators, seals and otters, 18 fish tanks of rare fish including leopard sharks, one tank of 1,200 small trout, a Japanese fishpond, and displays of mounted fish. Andrew Denison was the manager.

Plate 88 ~ Inside the rebuilt plunge there was a slide that ended with a splash in the pool. It was removed in 1919 for safety reasons. [Courtesy of University of California Santa Cruz Special Collections Library]

Plate 89 ~ The "women and children's" pool in the plunge, although there are some men in the pool in this picture. [Courtesy of University of California Santa Cruz Special Collections Library]

Bayshore Limited

The Bayshore Limited, the first entertainment train at the Boardwalk, ran from the Pleasure Pier to the mouth of the San Lorenzo River.[26] Opened in 1907, the train had an engine and six coaches, held 100 people, and had both an engineer and a fireman.

Fred Swanton *"talked Southern Pacific Railroad Company into giving him a five-coach special train to run to Nevada and back, stopping at various other*

Getting to the Beach

To get to the beach, people originally traveled by horse-drawn carriage on the "red line" and the "yellow line." One followed the Pacific Avenue narrow gauge rail track, and the other shared the Santa Cruz and Watsonville track down Chestnut Avenue. The line extended parallel to the rail tracks as far as the trestle over Water Street. (The concrete trestle was built in 1908. A metal plaque naming the Union Traction Company and John Martin, an important investor in the Boardwalk scheme, is still visible on the south railing.) Later, electric trolleys and then motorbuses departed from the beach every day at noon and took people to Pacific and Sycamore streets. Faster carriers served the Vue de L'Eau casino and took visitors to the Mission Hill hotels such as the Pope House and Bedell Hotel.

cities along the way to distribute souvenirs, streamers, and pamphlets advertising Santa Cruz as 'the Vacationer's Paradise.' He loaded these trains with two brass bands, a number of Santa Cruz civic leaders, and advertising men, and stopped at the city halls of various cities after parading up and down the streets to publicize the Boardwalk. They even held parties on the train, and gave away alcoholic beverages to advertise the merry, relaxed atmosphere that one could enjoy in Santa Cruz."[27] "Never A Dull Moment" became the post-fire slogan popularized by Swanton and accurately predicted the next few decades of Boardwalk history.

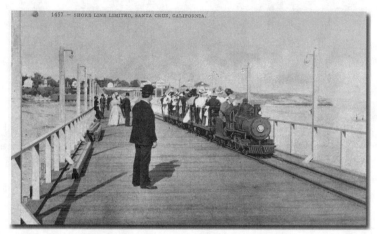

Plate 90 ~ Bay Shoire Limited miniature train. [Courtesy of the Harold J. van Gorder Collection]

Plate 91 ~ Bayshore Limited #23 miniature steam train, 1907. Built by Carney Brothers of New York. It ran from the east end of the Natatorium down the boardwalk, and through a sweeping tunnel near the river where it turned back towards the Natatorium. As a publicity stunt, the Santa Cruz Beach Railroad was incorporated and elaborate courtesy passes were sent to presidents of many railroads. On July 2, 1907, one of the senior executives of the Harriman Railroad in the East arrived with great fanfare and took the quick train ride as a guest of the Boardwalk. [Courtesy of the Harold J. van Gorder Collection]

Plate 92 ~ Summer on the beach. Electric Pier, train, ladies in summer dresses passing the Crazy House. Trestle continues to the right. [Courtesy of the Harold J. van Gorder Collection]

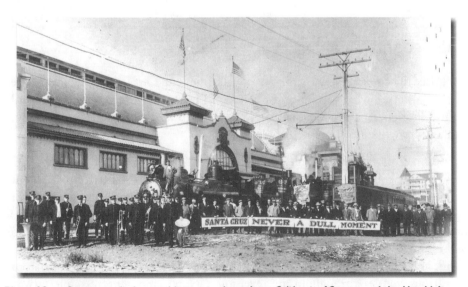

Plate 93 ~ Getting ready for a publicity trip throughout California. [Courtesy of the Harold J. van Gorder Collection]

Plate 94 ~ Fred Swanton, Fred Howe, and other "boosters". On a train trip to neighboring cities publicizing the attractions of the Boardwalk, about 1906. [Courtesy of University of California Santa Cruz Special Collections Library]

The Second Opening (1907-1914)

After the fire, the Santa Cruz Boardwalk re-opened for local citizens on June 3, 1907 offering what was billed as the second largest salt-water swimming pool on the west coast, a new Santa Cruz Casino ballroom, an upgraded Boardwalk, and an improved Pleasure Pier.

John Phillip Souza's band played to the crowds along with Queen Lil's orchestra, the Royal Hawaiians. Swanton received a telegram from President Teddy Roosevelt congratulating him on the event. The grand illumination of thousands of electric light bulbs outlining the buildings, windows, and railings took place at 8:00 p.m. after dinner was served in the grill room. The Casino orchestra led by Conrad Fuhrer, the Royal Hawaiian Sextet, the 22nd Infantry Band, and the Rink Band entertained, while the Santa Cruz Beach Band played in various venues throughout the evening. "Not a moment was idled away without music of some kind, interspersed with vocal selections." At 9 p.m. the Third Artillery Band began playing for the grand ball.

Plate 95 ~ Pacific Avenue 1907. [Courtesy of the Harold J. van Gorder Collection]

Plate 96 ~ Tourists, hotel representatives, and others greet the arriving train. Lots of cars. [Courtesy of the Harold J. van Gorder Collection]

Mermaids seen at Santa Cruz.

Plate 97 ~ "Mermaids seen at Santa Cruz," Postcard [Courtesy of the Harold van Gorder Collection]

The formal public opening was held on the anniversary of the 1906 fire, June 22, with coupons given to those entering the Casino. The *Santa Daily Cruz Surf* described it as "one of the greatest nights at the Santa Cruz Beach."[28] Charles Robinson of the Southern Pacific estimated 20-23,000 people attended that night.

Another formal opening appears to have been held around July 21. *"Festivities start at 8 p.m. with a "grand confetti battle," concerts by two bands, fireworks at 8:30 p.m., electrical illuminations, grand ball at 9 o'clock in the band room, music by full brass band, concert by the Strollers and Miss Brooks (soprano) in the grill room. The regular Saturday night admission to the ball will prevail, namely 50 cents."*[29] At 11 p.m. there was a drawing for prizes including bathing tickets, a Japanese beach shade parasol, dinner for four at the grill, and a lot in Swanton Beach Park valued at $500 (donated by Swanton).

THE SECOND OPENING

"The menu was:

Canapé of Caviar

Essence of Chicken Duchess

Olives

Radishes

Salted Almonds

Broiled Santa Cruz Bay Salmon

Potatoes Princess

Larded Tenderloin of Beef, Bouquetiere, fresh mushroom sauce

Sorbet of fine champagne

Roast Squab Chicken, au Cresson Julienne Potatoes

Fresh Crab Meat Salad, Casa Del Rey

Biscuit Tortoni

Petit Fours

Roquefort Cheese

Toasted Crackers

Coffee"

~ The Season is Opened. Santa Cruz Daily Surf, June 10, 1912, p1.1

Sentinel reporter Josephine Clifford McCrakin commented, *"The effect of the whole was dazzling; for every contour of the balconies and the great high windows, was outlined, bulb close upon bulb, in electric lights; the grand arches clearly defined, and above Old Glory waving slowly in the freeze. From the water it was Venice; but Venice never was illuminated like this."*[30]

The Santa Cruz Sentinel reported that many Santa Cruz citizens were overjoyed that the grand opening of the Boardwalk turned out to be such a success:

"The event was as though a great exposition was being opened. Tears were seen creeping unconsciously out of the eyes of many people, so overjoyed were they at realizing what a great step Santa Cruz had just taken from yesterday into today. A new epoch, a new era, greater prosperity – all these thoughts were ringing in the minds of the people so forcibly, that the people could not contain their feelings...."[31]

"The screech of the little train as it clatters by on the walk; the hum and whir of the concessions; the thunder and roar of the Scenic Railway, and the shouts of the riders; and rising above the din and the noise, the voice of the human megaphone, Charley Hagerdon: 'Big dance tonight in the Casino Ballroom, commencing at 9:15!'"[32]

The opening dinner at the Casino grill featured tables with flower centerpieces donated by the city's private clubs and some individuals. *"In the center was a table with a low brown wicker basket with the spreading azalea blooms. The dainty white harebell, with exquisite and rare ferns, proved to be a popular arrangement for a number of tables, while others were graced with the fragrant sweet peas, the choicest of roses, gladiolas and other beautiful blooms."*[33] Also present were soft lavenders of a rare orchid from John Martin's conservatory.

Plate 98 ~ The rebuilt Casino illuminated with thousands of electric lights. [Courtesy of University of California Santa Cruz Special Collections Library]

Plate 99 ~ Boardwalk in 191. [Courtesy of the Harold J. van Gorder Collection]

Plate 100 ~ Aerial beach scene, Pleasure Pier going to the right. The white building at the beginning of the pier was a J.W. Dickenson store that rented beach umbrellas. [Courtesy of the Harold van Gorder Collection]

Plate 101 ~ "Beautiful California – A Beach Scene on the Pacific On the Road of a Thousand Wonders. Notice the "Oriental" umbrellas. Postcard postmarked 1910. [Courtesy of the Harold van Gorder Collection]

Plate 102 ~ "On the Sands, Santa Cruz Beach, California. Notice the boys' striped bathing suits; these are the official rented suits. Postcard postmarked 1908. [Courtesy of the Harold van Gorder Collection]

The main appeal in these early years was strolling along the Boardwalk and pier, sitting on the sand, and a little ocean bathing, with swimming indoors and dining and dancing at night.

The first moving pictures in natural colors taken in America were shown in the Casino Theater March 20, 1912. "*They are of intense interest to all who keep abreast of the times, as they not only show the process of making this wonderful instrument of every business, the cash register, but also many of the latest inventions of modern science such as fireless locomotives, aero plane flights, improved methods of brass casting, etc. winding up with a series of views of the Panama Canal as it is at present. A lecturer accompanies the show, explaining every step as it is taken, the whole representing a vast expenditure of money and time on the part of the National Cash Register company and is given absolutely free to the citizens of Santa Cruz. A dance will be held afterwards for which an admission fee of 25c will be charged.*"[34]

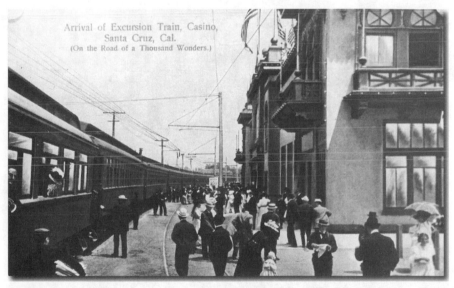

Plate 103 ~ So-called "excursion trains" allowed tourists to visit different spots in Santa Cruz and Monterey. The postcard says "On the Road of a Thousand Wonders". [Courtesy of the Harold J. van Gorder Collection]

By August crowds were again swarming to Santa Cruz. The *Santa Cruz Daily Surf* reported that 10,000 fares were taken in one day alone, and all of the hotels were full. The California Restaurant served 1,430 people one Sunday with other businesses similarly successful. "Every landlord will state that he turned away nearly as many as he sheltered." [35]

"I can remember way, way, way back when the popcorn wagons and the candy wagons were pulled down to the beach and it wasn't much of a Boardwalk. It really was an awfully nice place and the people who went there all dressed up in pretty clothes. There was a rotunda down there and if your family had the money, why, they rented a chair and sat in that rotunda. My father had his ideas of what was proper and correct and Fred Howe kind of leaned the other way. And so, they wanted enough people for this cracker-eating contest. I was down there looking up. I was only a little girl. I was up there watching and Fred Howe said, 'come on, come on.' And he pulled me up there on this platform ... and there was my family...well, I'd never taken part in one before, so I didn't know the more I jammed the crackers in my mouth, the more you can't swallow. My family was so mortified."[36]

"You could go into a place and for the price of admission you would spend all evening or all afternoon, for, I think, ten cents or a nickel, and you got on to this thing that spun around and spun around and then in the center, whoever, when all the others fell off, you got to ride. That was a lot of fun."[37]

Plate 104 ~ Crowded steps at the Casino. Postcard. [Courtesy of the Harold van Gorder Collection]

S. C. 116.   Casino, Santa Cruz, Cal.

Plate 105 ~ Casino. Postcard postmarked 1911. [Courtesy of the Harold van Gorder Collection]

Success Years

Thompson's Scenic Railway

In June 1908, L.A. Thompson's Scenic Railway was opened, the longest (1,050 feet) roller-coaster in the United States at the time.[38] L.A. Thompson was known as "The Father of Gravity" for inventing the roller-coaster in 1884. A Philadelphia Sunday school teacher, he was looking for more wholesome teen entertainment than the popular beer gardens. His idea came after visiting an abandoned coal mine where people paid five cents to coast down the shaft in gravity-powered coal cars. Thompson also built "The Switchback" at Coney Island, making $500 a day at five cents a head. It was so successful that competitors built two more coasters on Coney Island and another in San Francisco. Frederick Ingersoll, the largest manufacturer of park amusements, assisted Thompson in building the Boardwalk railway at a cost of $35,000. The attraction consisted of a four-minute, 25 mph 'diving and climbing' ride with undulating wooden hills, and two trains that paralleled each other with an engineer at the back. Each car held 30 people. The trains rolled on wooden tracks that paralleled the beach at the south end of the Boardwalk.

Plate 106 ~ The Thompson Scenic Railway. The railway consisted of a four-minute, 25 mph 'diving and climbing' train ride with undulating wooden hills (1908). [Courtesy of The Museum of Art & History@The McPherson Center, Santa Cruz, California]

Thompson's Scenic Railway was removed in 1924 to create space for the Giant Dipper.

It cost $3,900 to build what they called the "California Toboggan Ride," claiming you could "Slide Down the Hill Without Snow!" The 24-foot-high ride lasted 14 seconds and covered 500 feet of track, all for 10 cents. "All the sensation of being carried away by a cyclone." One reporter wrote: "The screams of the timid add to the excitement, but almost before a person is aware of it, he or she has reached the end of the track." The Californian Toboggan Ride lasted two summers until the sheriff served a writ of attachment for a debt of $140. The owner skipped town.

Before Thompson's Scenic Railway, the very first roller-coaster in Santa Cruz was built in 1884 by two Oakland promoters who built a circular track on Pacific Avenue, south of the present bus depot. The roller-coaster is to be located on the Hogdon lot, on the east side of Pacific Avenue opposite Maple Street. The outfit includes three car loads of freight, which arrived today. 5-21-1885 "The uprights of the roller-coaster are all in position and the prospects are that it will son be completed." 5-30-85 "Roller-coaster! Open for the Season. Will glide down hill from 10 a.m. to 10 p.m., Sundays excepted." July 15, 1885

Plate 107 ~ The popular Scenic Railway about 1908 (beach is to the right). This popular ride was located at the "end" of the boardwalk, close to the San Lorenzo River and where today's Giant Dipper roller-coaster ride stands. [Courtesy of Covello and Covello Collection]

Plate 108 ~ Early picture of the San Lorenzo River looking south towards the ocean. Trains continued to the right into the Boardwalk area. [Courtesy of the Harold J. van Gorder Collection]

The Balboa

April 1907 saw the arrival of the pleasure ship Balboa, anchored the summers of 1907-8 about 2,000 feet out from the Casino, and with a submarine cable to provide electricity. The large steam launch called the *Sinaloa* was the primary ship used to transport visitors to the *Balboa*.

The Balboa was originally built in Bath, Maine in 1874 and sailed as the J.B. Brown. She sailed around the Horn 25 times. In 1906 she was refitted in Oakland and re-christened the Balboa and moved to Santa Cruz.

" *The Balboa was a real three-masted, 207-foot ship which lay anchored opposite the Pleasure Pier. Launches conveyed tourists to and from the ship. Aboard, the visitors found a grill which featured seafood and music for dancing. At night the Balboa was emblazoned with over 3,000 colored lights. Also 'a huge search light' was mounted to attract still more attention.*"

A 180 x 40-foot shipboard ballroom on the second level featured nightly dancing but visitors could also dine, watch fireworks, play games of chance, or fish from the deck. The so-called "pleasure ship" was rumored to have many ways to satisfy tourists' desires. Years later on March 15, 1914 her owners let her sink in the San Francisco bay after setting fire to her.

359 – THE "BALBOA", WITH LAUNCH "SINALOA", SANTA CRUZ HARBOR.

Plate 109 ~ The pleasure ship Balboa. With the launch Sinaloa in the Santa Cruz Harbor. Around 1907. [Courtesy of the Harold J. van Gorder Collection]

In June 1908 Swanton arranged for the American Kennel Club dog show to be held at the Boardwalk. Closing day of the dog show was opening day of the 1908 season. That opening featured the usual dinner, dancing, and fireworks events, plus two star entertainers, Cluff and Embree, who were ragtime pianists. Swanton also installed a long-promised bronze public drinking fountain that year on the esplanade at the west entrance to the Casino building.

May 1, 1908 started Fleet Week with 45 ships in the area and saw the opening of the "new idea" dance pavilion in the "transformed" skating rink area. The floor was pure white and smooth with wax. New electrical lights and an adjoining ice cream parlor complemented the space. Kenneth Wise was the floor manager with dancing starting at 9 p.m. The 22nd Infantry Band provided the music. After a successful one-week trial period the pavilion was closed until the official opening in June.

The 1908 season also saw the opening of a new German restaurant managed by Mr. Conlisk. The 50 x 150-foot building could seat 500 people and came complete with 20 young women in German costumes. A $9,000 organ was installed to provide music.

Plate 110 ~ Flagship Connecticut (center). Admiral "Fighting Bob" Evans Great White Fleet visits Santa Cruz in an around-the-world goodwill cruise 1908. [Courtesy of the Harold J. van Gorder Collection]

One way to get a sense of how busy the Boardwalk area was is to look at the 1908 "weekend program of entertainment" proposed by F.W. Swanton.[39]

May 8 and 9 — Afternoon and evening concerts at the Casino.

May 15 and 16 — Afternoon and evening concerts at the Casino.

May 18 — Grand Skating Carnival

May 22 and 23 — Afternoon and evening concerts at the Casino.

May 30 and 31 — Afternoon and evening concerts at the Casino.

June 5 and 6 — Afternoon and evening concerts at the Casino with special feature ball on Saturday night the 5th.

June 12 — Grand summer opening of the Casino with a ball and night fireworks, confetti battle, special dinner.

June 19 — Grand Carnival and ball

June 20 — Daylight fire works, aquatic sports and games at the beach

June 26 — Grand comical nose ball and confetti battle, band concerts, and fireworks

June 26-28 — Opening of Swanton Beach Park, special trains coming in from all over the state

June 27 — Paper Balloon Day (hot air balloons by the hundreds), band concerts, dancing

July 3 and 4 — Fourth of July celebration, flag day, sports on the beach, swimming races, balloon ascension, fireworks, flag ball and dinner.

July 10 and 11 — Balloon carnival (thousands of toy balloons with pictures of the beach and surrounding scenery), grand balloon dinner and dancing, band concert.

July 17 — Grand masquerade ball and confetti battle.

July 22, 23, 24 — Baby show and grand ball.

July 29 week — Yacht clubs invited to Santa Cruz, boat races during the week.

July 31 — Cascaroni ball, games, aquatic sports

August 7 and 9vAnnual Mardi Gras festival

August 11 — Comic costume skating carnival

August 14 and 15 — Confetti battle and duster carnival

August 21 — Blowout night and comic costume ball

August 28 — Confetti battle and squawker night, grand ball, band concert.

Sept 4 and 5 — Grand ball and Labor Day celebration

Sept 9, 10, 11 — Admission Day carnival.

Events such as hot air balloon ascensions and boxing matches kept crowds interested. On July 5, 1909, a 10-year-old boy became entangled in the balloon's trailing rope. Aeronaut Virgil Moore managed to reach him and held both tightly to the ropes. They moved about 800 yards out over the bay and 500 feet up when the balloon began to loose gas. Eventually they sank into the water and were rescued by the cruiser *Alert*.

In 1911 Swanton complained to the City Council that *"people in bathing suits were lounging in the sands amidst the [guests]. He has placed signs on the beach to prohibit objectionable habits among the bathers so as to confine them within certain limits. There is plenty of room near the water's edge and also east of the pier and west of the band stand."* [40] He didn't want to share the sand with unpaid guests.

Looff's Carousel

The carousel has always been one of the Boardwalk's most popular attractions. Delivered on August 3, 1911 by its creator, Charles I.D. Looff, it was considered a "thrill" ride at the time. Looff was born in Denmark on May 24, 1852. He immigrated to New York in 1870 and was soon employed as a furniture carver. In his spare time, Looff carved his first carousel horse in his attic using scrap wood from the factory. He sold the piece to Coney Island immediately, originating what would later become known as the Coney Island style.

Looff built about forty carousels in all, many in New York and Rhode Island, and several along the West Coast. The Boardwalk carousel is one of only nine operating Looff carousels today, with others in Yerba Buena Center, San Francisco and Spokane, Washington.

After placing several carousels in the western United States, Looff and his wife, Anna, moved in 1912 to Long Beach, California where he set up his factory. The couple lived on the second floor of the factory until Looff died in 1918.

Plate 111 ~ Looff's Merry-Go-Round. This is a fairly recent picture and shows the carousel housed in the 1960 building that replaced the original structure. The carousel itself has virtually the same look as it did when installed in 1911. [Courtesy of the Harold J. van Gorder Collection]

Looff's middle initials, "I.D.," came about when Ellis Island officials told him he had to have a middle name "for his I.D." Looff's sense of humor and personality show in his hand-carved horses. Several of the Boardwalk's carousel horses display their teeth in open smiles, a gentle, playful look in contrast to the stern faces popular in European roundabouts. A single rosette carved on the breast of each horse is Looff's signature mark. Each horse is unique and colorfully detailed. Many are decorated with swords at their sides or garlands of flowers around their necks. Faux jewels emblazon their saddles. The tails are crafted from real horse hair.

Plate 112 ~ Riding the Carousel – 1950s? [Courtesy of the Covello and Covello Collection]

The art of carving carousel horses the way Looff did has almost disappeared. Because of their rarity, carousel horses have become collectible and increasingly valuable. The Boardwalk's entire carousel cost $18,000 in 1911. Today just one of the Looff horses could bring in excess of that if sold; the carousel is worth over $350,000.

The carousel is home to 73 horses who ride four abreast. Seventy-one of those are jumpers, horses that go up and down without their feet touching the platform. There are also two Roman chariots decorated with the heads of rams and cherubs. All of the horses are original Looff horses, with ten replacement horses that were brought in during a restoration in the 1980s from parks in Myrtle Beach, South Carolina and Belmont Park, San Diego.

The Seaside Company has restored many of the horses and continues to do so. Each must be chemically stripped of all paint, sometimes down to their original white and gold color. The next step is to repair legs, knees, surface holes, or cracks in the wood by using dowels and wood fillers. In many cases, the horses' saddles, knees, and other areas that are subject to rough wear are coated with fiberglass for added protection. Worn details, such as decorated saddles and manes, are re-carved or rebuilt with wood putty prior to sanding and painting. Ongoing maintenance includes touching up worn or chipped paint, mechanical adjustments and repairs, and frequent polishing of the ride's many brass poles and ornate mirrors. Restoration is an expensive process costing about $2,000 per horse, but is as much a preservation of history as the refurbishment of an amusement park ride.

The Santa Cruz carousel is also one of only a handful of carousels in the world still featuring a working "gold" ring dispenser, although the rings are now all steel. Riders try to grab a ring as they ride by and a ring, tossed into a canvas clown target, is good for one free ride on the carousel. Workers fed rings into the "arm" until the early 1950s when it was mechanized. Steel replaced the brass rings in the 1970s because the brass interfered with the ride's electronic stop and start device. The Boardwalk replaces 85,000 rings annually, as patrons walk off with souvenirs of their ride on the carousel. You can even occasionally find people selling the rings on eBay!

The canvas clown was retired in 1958. Ridership dropped 75 percent, so the Boardwalk brought the rings and clown back immediately and he has reigned ever since.

Music for the carousel comes from the 342-pipe Ruth and Sohn band organ built in 1894. The German-made machine is one of the last of its kind. When it was renovated in 1979, many of the parts had to be handmade.

The carousel was originally housed in a structure built in 1911. In October 1960 the building was demolished and rebuilt. The new $100,000 building was designed by Ronald A. White of Beverly Hills, a noted amusement industry architect.

Half a million people ride the carousel each year. In 1987, the U.S. Park Service declared the ornate merry-go-round a National Historic Landmark, along with the Giant Dipper roller-coaster.

Casa Del Rey

To try and capture "the prestigious and wealthy," Swanton built a new luxury hotel across from the Casino. Work on the Casa del Rey (House of the King) began in 1910 at the corner of Cliff and Beach streets. Swanton, John Martin, and other partners began the new ultra-modern "fire-proof Kahn concrete system" hotel directly across from the Casino in the former cottage area. Remember this was only four years after the devastating 1906 San Francisco earthquake and fire safety was a significant issue to visitors. Fred R. Cummings was hired to move the cottages eastward. George Applegarth was asked to be the overall architect. Rickon & Ehrhart of San Francisco were winning bidders on the construction, Heath & Faneuf of Santa Cruz on plumbing, Cox Electric, then new, on the electrical elements.

Plate 113 ~ Building the Casa del Rey hotel 1910-11. Taken from the Casino roof. [Courtesy of University of California Santa Cruz Special Collections Library]

"The long rectangular hotel is of a Spanish style design with Pueblo-style projecting rafters, known as 'vigas' [and] a Mission Revival segmental roofline. The hotel is three stories high with a 100,000 square foot footprint. It has a symmetrical layout originally planned to have two interior courts. The front wall is accented with four unornamented columns above the main entrance and with brick red trim to delineate the roofline and the vigas." [41]

"The Casa del Rey was in the shape of a hollow rectangle, fronting 335 feet on Cliff Street and 135 feet on Beach Street. 300 rooms, 200 with connecting baths. Within the hotel courts are two Italian gardens, each 100 x 55 feet, opening from the main lobby. Each room in the hotel has a private telephone connection and is furnished with the richest of furniture, carpets, curtains and pictures. The lobby of the hotel is in two sections, making one grand lobby of 60 x 120 feet. At the east end is a fireplace of original construction, the mantel of which is twelve feet across. The electric passenger elevators carry guests to the sleeping apartments in the upper stories of the hotel. The wide, heavily carpeted corridors extending around the building measure 800 feet in length, making a promenade of six and a half laps to the mile. A graceful and strongly constructed bridge connecting Casa del Rey with the Casino leading into the grill room links the two superb buildings together as virtually one." [42]

The hotel also had a fine restaurant and tennis court, wonderful gardens, and nightly entertainment events for the estimated 1,000 guests. About 200 of the moved cottages remained for those wanting less expensive quarters.

Plate 114 ~ Casa del Rey and Casino drawing. Postcard with 1912 postmark. [Courtesy of the Harold J. van Gorder Collection]

In the March 9, 1911 issue of the *Sentinel,* John Martin, president of the Santa Cruz Beach Company, stated, "To promote the integrity of these facilities the hotel was painted the same color, a light cream color, to harmonize with the casino and the Natatorium (a.k.a. the Plunge) as much as possible."

Work was scheduled for completion by May 1, 1911, and the first group, the Grand Parlors of the Native Sons & Native Daughters of the Golden West, arrived June 1. The official opening occurred Saturday, June 3, 1911, along with the seasonal opening of the Boardwalk. Casa del Rey cost approximately $500,000 to build. In 1911 the *Santa Cruz Daily Surf* reported that Casa del Rey had every room occupied or engaged. That year they had a budget of $18,000 for advertising, illumination, music, and fireworks.

"The Casa del Rey featured a beautiful lounge with a dance hall, the Rose Room, and a dining room serving fine meals. A unique overhead walkway with windows, soft carpets, and a tile roof, joined the hotel and the casino, so advertisers could boast that one could have 'everything under one roof' in Santa Cruz. In front of the hotel was a large garden with exotic palm trees and colorful flowers, and a number of footpaths leading to the hotel and casino entrances."

Plate 115 ~ Casa del Rey postcard about 1919. [Courtesy of the Harold J. van Gorder Collection]

Plate 116 ~ Sun Room at the Casa del Rey. Postcard [Courtesy of the Harold J. van Gorder Collection]

Plate 117 ~ Casino from the esplanade. Restaurant on the left, bridge over the railroad tracks connecting the hotel to the second floor of the Casino. From a 1914 color postcard. [Courtesy of the Harold J. van Gorder Collection]

Plate 118 ~ Casa del Rey hotel. Notice the number of parked automobiles. [Courtesy of University of California Santa Cruz Special Collections Library]

Plate 119 ~ Lobby of the Casa del Rey. [Courtesy of University of California Santa Cruz Special Collections Library]

In 1911 F.A. Hihn sued the City of Santa Cruz and the Union Traction Company (railroads) claiming that he owned the now highly desirable beach land between Main Street and Cliff Street, originally sold to him by the California Powder Works in 1887, which had been given to the Powder Works by the City. The City countered that it owned the beach property under a California 1872 act granting all beach lands "for the benefit of the public." Much of the testimony revolved around early citizens' recollections about where the ocean tides reached in those earlier days. After Hihn lost the suit he offered to deed some of the land back to the City so it could be used for streets and walkways in the area so that "he could leave the world in peace."

Water Carnival - Revived

On July 20, 1912, one month after the famous Sea Beach Hotel was destroyed by fire, a new water pageant was held trying to revive interest in the beach area. It was advertised as "Nine big days of glorious pageantry," reminiscent of the Venetian Water Carnivals that were held in Santa Cruz in the 1890s. The pageant was centered on the river island at the last bend of the San Lorenzo River.

Miss Clara Walti was selected as Queen, with runner-ups Veda Smith and Frances Richards. The beauty pageant was held opening night and Josephine Clifford McCrackin reported in the next day's morning *Sentinel*: *"A spectacle to be proud of, most picturesque and romantic. Thousands of lights across the river where the reflection fell on the water were lights of many colors. Music over the waters floating dreams of glitter and tinsel moving on the bosom of the river. Neptune himself in a huge seashell drawn by his seahorses . [Mayor George W. Stone] addressed the crowd. The queen rules our hearts and in our homes. The mother, the wife, the sister are all Queen in their own right. It is thereof fitting that we should choose one of our city's fairest daughters to preside over the festivities of the coming week. "*[43]

The last water carnival was held in 1927 but Skip Littlefield kept the spirit alive in the Plunge Water Carnivals of the 1930s. Capitola began the Begonia Festival in 1954 on the same premise.

The Boardwalk increased its normal evening illumination and created a special path to the festivities. Every night there were special shows, from a seven-act vaudeville show to grand opera by the Grassi Opera Company, who presented *Pinafore* featuring several local singers, including Milton Watson who later became a Broadway star. A parade of floats on the river was held nightly before the shows. *"The act of the Hadji troupe with its 'whirling dervish' and Sherif, the Mohammedan dancer, the Arabian acrobats and gun spinners, is well remembered."*[44]

Decline (1913)

Since the opening of the Boardwalk, trains were the way most visitors came to the area so most elected to stay for long periods of time, even all summer. Times were about to change. Automobile prices came down and sales were increasing. Gas was cheaper than the price of summer boarding and people with automobiles looked for bargain day trip opportunities instead of renting places to stay.

Then suddenly the town was startled by the news that the Beach Company was considering bankruptcy, saying that the declining number of tourists, less spending per tourist, and a minor economic depression in the country had simply made it impossible to continue operations. Other local businessmen were suffering economic decline but they were even more frightened by the implications of the loss of the Boardwalk business.

The year 1913 saw three wagons "loaded high with bathing suits" being sold to the Gaba and Magidson company for rags.[45] A new visitors' information booth, sponsored by the Chamber of Commerce, was setup to help induce visitors to stay in the town and visit more attractions. Local women staffed the booth, answered questions, and advertised both local attractions and the economic health of the area. Times were hard.

Plate 120 ~ Sea Beach Hotel on the right. Lynch House is in the far background. Electric trolley and band members on the beach. Picture around 1910. [Courtesy of the Harold J. van Gorder Collection]

Plate 121 ~ Ready for an ocean plunge. October 1913. Third girl on the left was Verel Shannon, "the girl that I married in 1925," reports Harold van Gorder. [Courtesy of the Harold J. van Gorder Collection]

Restarting The Boardwalk, Again

John Martin, President of the failing Santa Cruz Beach Company told local businessmen in early 1914 that it was unlikely the Boardwalk would be able to open for the summer, although the Casa del Rey was scheduled to open on May 27th. On May 26, 1914 the *Santa Cruz Daily Surf* reported that Ralph.S. Miller, Boardwalk Manager, and four other local citizens had offered to take over management of the Casino. John Tait of Tait-Zinkland and Otto Mueller (both of San Francisco) who ran the grill, bar and cafeteria the previous year also made an offer. The *Sentinel* newspaper ran a front page story saying that only local businessmen should be considered. The *Sentinel* though that the two San Francisco based businessmen, while qualified, were too "Bohemian for some of us, a little too much like San Francisco....Local businessmen would be more concerned with their long term local reputation and would do a better job." [46]

A day later the *Surf* and *Sentinel* newspapers announced that the Casino, Casa Del Rey, Natatorium, Cottage City, and all attractions except for the parking garage had been leased for the 1914 season through early September to J.J.C.

Leonard (Hotel St. George and the Sea Beach Hotel), C.E. Towne (grocery businessman), and Edgar Wilson (former Beach Company accountant), all of Santa Cruz, and that they hoped to find additional investors. The rumored price was $12,000. The timing was good because the city had turned off the water to those facilities because the Beach Company bill hadn't been paid. Plans were immediately made to reopen facilities and the next day an official announcement headlined the local papers "Confidence is Restored in Santa Cruz." [47] The actual vote by stockholders was apparently a foregone conclusion because they weren't scheduled to meet until August 6th when the season would be half over.

Plate 122 ~ In September 1914 Ralph .S. Miller, Boardwalk Manager and four other citizens offered to take over management of the Casino from the failing company. This picture was taken later in 1940. [Courtesy of University of California Santa Cruz Special Collections Library]

A special new asbestos curtain and stage scenery were installed in the Casino Theater in 1914 and a contract was let to the American Vacuum Cleaning Company for a complete cleaning of the interior. A new electrical automatic shooting gallery and a miniature trolley car "in which travelers can visit through a series of views all the wonders of the world"[48] completed the attractions.

In the summer of 1914 a new attraction was started at the Boardwalk: free evening movies. A temporary screen was hung across the bandstand at night. The Igorote village of head-hunters from the Philippine Islands arrived as part of the entertainment, living in tents on the beach. June 20 was the official opening where 450 people enjoyed a formal dinner in the main grill. Music and fireworks followed. Although overall attendance was low there was guarded optimism about the future.

Carl Sword was the Casa del Rey manager (he used to manage the Sea Beach Hotel before the big fire). D.J. Riordan was the assistant manager.

The Municipal Wharf was dedicated on December 5, 1914, using $165,000 from a bond election. The Steamship *Roanoke* anchored off the wharf for the inaugural festivities, unloading autos, pianos, linoleum, and other freight. Capt. R. Rickson attended a big luncheon put together by local ladies, and E.D. Rockwell, the new wharf master, spoke of the promise for revenue coming from the new wharf. Three thousand people attended the event. Boardwalk management saw the wharf as a tourist draw from which they would benefit.

Plate 123 ~ S.S. Roanoke. Dedication of the Santa Cruz Municipal Wharf, December 5, 1914. S.S. Roanoke tied up alongside for the occasion. [Courtesy of the Harold J. van Gorder Collection]

Plate 124 ~ S.S. Roanoke docked alongside the municipal wharf. [Courtesy of the Harold J. van Gorder Collection]

Another Bankrupcy

Just when things began to look encouraging, the revived Beach Company declared bankruptcy in late 1914 and the buildings were again closed. With the increasing popularity of the auto, tourists spent less time and money in Santa Cruz and failed to *"form the kind of attachment and feel that their predecessors had. The tourist became a more anonymous entity."* [49] The bottom line was that revenues did not support the cutback operations. The future looked bleak.

"Prior to its 1915 summer season opening, the Santa Cruz Beach Company was bankrupt. Its assets consisted only of its property holdings. According to one source, John Martin – the primary financier of the beach enterprises – was also bankrupt. Consequently 'money dried up' around Santa Cruz and beach buildings were boarded up." [50]

Local businesses were greatly concerned about the effect of repeated openings and closings on public perception and Mayor Fred R. Howe asked for volunteers to prepare the buildings for a possible 1915 season. Meanwhile local officials tried to find new sources of investment.

The Seaside Company

Seaside Company Buys Assets (1916)

On February 25, 1916, Articles of Incorporation were filed creating the Santa Cruz Seaside Company, based initially in San Francisco. The Board of Trustees were Edward M. Lind, Edward Fox, and J. Brockhoff, all of San Francisco. Seventy thousand dollars of capital stock were issued with the largest stockholder being Hotaling Estate Company ($7,800). Many Santa Cruz residents also purchased stock.[51]

A parallel organization, the Beach Hotel Company, was incorporated at the same time with trustees Allan Pollack, Edward Fox, and Edward M. Lind. Capital stock for that company was $300,000 held by R.L. Wiley ($2000); Southern Pacific Company ($100,000); Grant Company, Sloss Securities Company, and Hotaling Estate Company ($64,000); S. Waldo Coleman ($4,000); John Martin ($163,200); Sloss Securities Company ($15,000); F.W. Swanton ($3,000); Granite Rock Company ($1,800); Allan Pollock ($5,000); Edward Fox ($1,000); and Edward M. Lind ($1,000).[52]

Plate 125 ~ S. Waldo Coleman. Santa Cruz Seaside Company & Beach Hotel Company President 1916-1928. [Courtesy of The Museum of Art & History@The McPherson Center, Santa Cruz, California]

S. Waldo Coleman, Manager of the Union Traction Company and Coast Counties Gas and Electric, was confirmed as Manager of the new company for the 1916 season, a move that was popularly received by Santa Cruz citizens. His management team now controlled the Casino, Natatorium, Casa Del Rey, Cottage City, and the Boardwalk.

The *Santa Cruz Daily Surf* reported in April 1916 that, *"It is understood that F. W. Swanton, Henry Willey, F.R. Walti, H.E. Irish, George Staffler and other local original stockholders in the Beach Company have [completely] disposed of their interest [in Boardwalk activities], and that with them beach management will only be a memory. Those were gallant days when the first Casino was constructed; both times and men have changed."* [53]

The Santa Cruz Seaside Company's first permanent directors were Samuel Leask, A. A. Morey, W.S. Moore, J.R. Williamson, and George A. Montell, selected in April 1916. The new organization attempted to establish clear responsibilities, believing that the Chamber of Commerce and City Council held the ultimate responsibility for bringing people to Santa Cruz and making that experience pleasurable. The Boardwalk team would be part of that effort but the team was solely focused on making the Boardwalk itself a profitable venture.

Mayor F.R. Howe declared June 3, 1916 to be a "half day holiday" so that local people could celebrate at the beach as part of an official "Clean up! Open up!" campaign to ready the area for visitors. At noon most businesses closed and long tables were set up on the beach enabling them to seat 800 at a time for lunch. Two thousand pounds of sole were grilled over coal fires and local merchants donated coffee, boiled eggs, and other food. Band music was provided and, of course, all the local politicians showed up. That evening, children from Branciforte School, under the direction of Miss Iris Mitchell, did folk dancing demonstrations and later a grand ball was held in the Casino ballroom.

The 1916 season officially opened with a large party at the Casino. Casa del Rey and Cottage City had 450 arrivals and a special excursion train from San Jose brought 200 people who spent the day at the beach. The vice president of Southern Pacific, E.O. McCormack, parked his private train car nearby and attended the "brilliant banquet and ball" official opening. As usual, local parties purchased tables for their friends and family, each uniquely decorated with flowers. Ballroom dancing and concert music followed. Local papers covered the event in detail, listing many society members who attended.

After the success of 1916, businesses opened the 1917 season with high hopes. The early May crowds were greater than expected, with most being weekend auto parties, including motorcyclists. The improving roads made the journey easier and the novelty of automobiles made trips to the Santa Cruz beach popular.

The 1917 season opened officially on June 30 with a formal early dinner for 700 at the Casino grill. Interestingly this was a page four article in local newspapers, the season openings no longer being a dominant front page event. Crowds continued, however, and R.S. Miller reported that 2,721 Natatorium tickets had been sold to bathers on July 4 alone. A new bowling alley also attracted visitors. Glass now enclosed the space of the rotunda under the grill and the ice cream parlor was moved to this area. The cafeteria in the Casino was painted white, adding "light and cheer" to the large room.

Professor Karnoh came to the city for the 1917 season and worked in the Casino. He had visited twice previously and attracted crowds at his lectures and personal readings. He considered himself an expert in palmistry, astrology, and phrenology and was a popular fixture at the Boardwalk.

Harold van Gorder remembers working in the cafeteria in 1917. *"Except for the chef, the staff was made up of locals: wives of a business man and a street railway motorman; a quiet reserved, kindly lady the gossips labeled a former "kept" person of a prominent businessman; and some high school girls. There was also a dissipated ex-infantry man who had served in China during the Boxer Rebellion. The cafeteria public entrance was to the left inside the Casino doorway off Beach Street. Service facilities were on the alley between the Casino and the Natatorium. The union scale for this work was $40 per week; my wage $10. Hours: come early, leave when you're through. Benefits: "found meals."*[54]

The Boardwalk was back on its feet, and the 1918 Fourth of July weekend drew huge crowds. The weather was magnificent and the *Surf* reported that, *"The beach was a kaleidoscope of color as every parasol from the curio store was rented and those on the beach gave a vivid color scheme to those who watched the bathers and listened to the band concerts."*[55] Never were there so many autos along the beach front and adjoining streets. During the day nearly 1,900 people used the Natatorium, besides hundreds of locals who came directly from home to the beach. Every concession did outstanding business and most cottages, including the Casa del Rey, were full throughout the season.

Parking was becoming an issue with the growing popularity of the automobile. J.B. Bird opened a new auto park at a cost of $15,000 making it the greatest improvement in the beach area that year. The auto park could handle 400 cars "left in perfect safety" and was bounded by Riverside Avenue, Beach, and River streets. Within the lot there was an auto "supply station" with a self-service, coin-operated gasoline and oil pump. Women had a furnished restroom with a hair-drying facility.

Bookings and crowds continued throughout the summer making this one of the most successful seasons in years. A new branch of the city library was opened at the Casino and the *Santa Cruz Daily Surf* reported that in the first month 125 visitors had paid a deposit fee so they could have library privileges.

"Chief Hannah and Officer Baxter had a busy day Sunday at the beach arranging a parking system. They allowed no autos to be parked south of the railroad tracks and a long white line was drawn 12 feet north of the S.P. tracks, thus keeping all autos that distance away from the tracks. There were about as many cars parked Sunday as on the Fourth. They reached on Beach Street from Westbrook to beyond Raymond Street with every side street lined with machines. The new Bird parking station was crowded, as were all the beach garages." ~ *Auto Parking at the Beach. Santa Cruz Daily Surf*, July 8 1918, p.3.

A GAME of SCIENCE and SKILL .... THE BEST DRIVER WINS

Plate 126 ~ Auto race game at the Boardwalk about 1920. [Courtesy of the Harold J. van Gorder Collection]

By the following year, an editorial by George Stone waxed that, "At no previous period in its history has the future of the city taken on such a hopeful aspect as today."[56] There were 68 Southern Pacific coaches arriving for the Fourth of July. The following Saturday there were even more people to the point that patrons had to double up at the Natatorium. "So great

Advertisement in the Sentinel June 1919: "Dance, Casino Ball Room, Saturday Evening June 7th, Doctors agree, we believe, that dancing is one of the best forms of exercise for the stimulation of the blood circulation." ~ Dance. Advertisement, *Santa Cruz Sentinel*, June 6, 1919, p.2.

was the crush getting [swimming] suits that the crowds went up against and broke one of the windows in the suit department. Manager Miller announces that yesterday's crowd was the largest ever at the Plunge." [57]

CASINO AND PLEASURE PIER
W-41   SANTA CRUZ, CALIFORNIA

Plate 127 ~ Casino and Pleasure Pier, speed boats, and a water skiier. Undated postcard. [Courtesy of the Harold J. van Gorder Collection]

"New attractions: It is a U.S. recruiting station on the Boardwalk, with Sergt. A. Kuhn in charge, who has two assistants, and all three are the most peace loving of men. They invite all those so inclined to enter the army, and they have a lot of war trophies, machine guns and elements to show what war is. However the sergeant and his assistants have the regulation bronze and silver buttons for distribution to those who earned them. And the sergeant has expressed the opinion that there will be two airplanes here in the course of this day to help celebrate the Fourth. And don't forget that a brand new whale has been caught, and is on exhibition." [58]

"When you enter the Casino you become a summer visitor, though you had been here and lived here all your life. It is a different world you enter, lighting up Sallee's international arcade, the Japanese Tree Tea garden and the Lemos painting gallery, the greater curio establishment, the kewpie embroidery stand, the gargoyle circle, the stationery establishment; all these together have a slightly bewildering effect and you know just exactly how a stranger, entering here for the first time, would feel. Music floats in from the Venice side of the Casino, the Jennings Seaside Band on the beach bandstand; and music floats out from the Casino Arcade Orchestra…year after year we find friends again on the promenade and Boardwalk; and season after season we

hear the glad yells of the swimmers in the Plunge, and hear the shouts of the travelers on the scenic railway whose lights seem constantly on the move, for the train seldom stands still. Light streams from the wide open doors of the merry-go-round; and looking back one sees light dancing on the waters of the bay....and now the ball is on. The Casino ballroom filled with the youthful forms that follow the rhythm of the music furnished under the direction of Fred Jennings himself." [59]

During the July 4, 1919 week, "every hotel and lodging house in town has been full for three nights. The Cottage City had to turn away about 700, and many slept on the beach all night."[60] The *Santa Cruz Evening News* estimated over 20,000 visitors and 2,115 cars had arrived for the weekend. There was a three-hour backup on the highway coming into Santa Cruz due to a motorists' breakdown. *"Automobiles lined the sidewalks for three and four blocks from the beach front during yesterday afternoon, every available foot of space being taken. The crowd yesterday afternoon literally swarmed over Santa Cruz beach from the municipal pier to the San Lorenzo River. There was hardly a square yard of vacant sand in front of the Casino properties in the middle of yesterday afternoon... the Casino ballroom dances last night were packed with patrons and the Casino grill did an enormous business all day long."*[61] Street car lines alone handled up to 18,000 every day.

"Near beer" in beer bottles was a new addition at the Casino bar. A new Rainier "soft but satisfying" drink was especially popular with the ladies. *"I just think it's great that we can step up to the bar and elbow up with the good fellows who are talking all about the big things in the world. Why a girl learns more in half an hour about the world's doings in a barroom than she could gain in reading a whole newspaper. I've always craved to be able to get inside a barroom and have the liberty of staying as long as I pleased without feeling that I was breaking the law, and now the time has arrived and I'm just going to have a swell time this summer and lift a few high ones over the bar with my girl friends when they arrive next week to spend a month's vacation here."*[62] Charles Pimentel and Bill Watters were the bartenders.

The now annual arrival of the navy fleet brought many curious visitors. Beverino & Perez were asked by the city to coordinate bringing visitors out to the fleet ships. They contracted with Crowley for four launch boats that made constant shuttle trips from the municipal pier. Pete Silva and Louis Carnaglia of the Western California Fish Company brought the 300-passenger steamer *Christopher Columbus* down from San Francisco for the summer to add additional capacity and Cottardo Stagnaro had 40 seats put into one of his launches.

A "flying boat" arrived in July, piloted by Dan Davidson. Famous Aviator Earl C. Cooper was the primary pilot and was well-known for scenic flights over the San Francisco Bay and his participation in movies. Based in San Francisco he planned to spend the summer in Santa Cruz as long as demand existed. The boat anchored in the bay and offered scenic or stunt flights to waiting passengers. A few days later *"two passengers, a man and a woman, flying with Pilot Dan Davidson in his big seaplane yesterday afternoon, were given a thrill seldom accorded the seekers of sensations in the air when the propeller of the flying boat broke in half when the ship was about 500 feet above the bay off Del Mar, and a sudden shoot to safety was made in a hair-raising glide to a point just beyond the breaker line off Twin Lakes. No one was hurt but the passengers will not forget the drop for many a day to come. A launch from Santa Cruz was soon on the spot and towed the damaged plane to its anchorage off the casino."* [63]

Repair work on the Glenwood Highway (later 17) was announced but Fred Howe was concerned that the construction would negatively impact tourism the summer of 1920. Arrangements were made with the contractor to complete work from Los Gatos to the summit before summer so that tourists could then cross over to Old San Jose Road to get to Santa Cruz.

In mid-April 1920 the Natatorium opened for the season but throngs of visitors found a series of new rules including: *"Bathers must first take a shower before they go in the Plunge, and use soap if necessary as the Plunge 'is not a bath tub.' Those who have private suits must have them properly laundered [and] women in the Plunge must wear caps."* [64]

The annual July 4, 1920 celebration began at 10 a.m. with patriotic singing of "America the Beautiful" and the "Star Spangled Banner", afternoon aquatic and athletic sports at the beach so that spectators could watch, and the usual ball and fireworks in the evening. The Santa Cruz Evening News reported that 3,000 visitors had found rooms with the help of the Chamber of Commerce and that "every available room in Santa Cruz was brought into use."[65] The News article also reported that the Chamber of Commerce had successfully managed to ensure enough gasoline was available in town for visitors' automobiles. And not too different from today, a motorist had broken down near the summit on Highway 17, blocking the road until 11 p.m. Sunday evening.

Auto safety was an issue even in 1920. The News reported on July 8 that "Even with the rush of auto travel, before and after the Fourth, the speed maniac was not to be held in check. Officer Griffin reported arrests totaled 29." J.T. Shoptaw of Stockton was arrested for speeding more than 35 miles an hour on Glenwood Highway, Bill Arnly of Bakersfield for not carrying two lighted lamps on the front of his car, and J.C. Jercovich of Watsonville for not having the spot light arranged according to law. "One can just guess what might have been the death and accident toll without rigid enforcement of the law."

A new "highest class" grocery opened just east of the Natatorium along with the Spanish restaurant operated by Mrs. Jones; the Cow Hayes alleys, Rosyse and Frank, popcorn and candy; Cox & McClintic cigars; J.W. Dickson curio stand, and the penny arcade. Miller, "the hot dog king," opened his waffle, hot dog, and sandwich stand. Another improvement in late 1920 was installation of a 90-ton filtering plan at the Natatorium to improve capacity and water clarity.

Plate 128 ~ Hot Dog Miller's stand about 1934. [Courtesy of University of California Santa Cruz Special Collections Library]

Haswell Leask reported in an interview that his father Samuel had been asked by Waldo Coleman (Coast County Gas and Electric) to be a director in the new corporation. He agreed but had little interest in the business. When Samuel died his family discovered stock in the Seaside Company that he had purchased at $6 per share was now worth $700 per share. The family gave the money to various community groups. Samuel had a pass to the Boardwalk but *"He never allowed his sons or daughters to use that pass. He said if you want to go for that foolishness you earn the money. Well, that was the case, we never used the pass. But when the grandchildren came along, why boy, he'd ask my mother 'Where's that Seaside pass?.'"* [66]

Plate 129 ~ Leask's Seaside Store (on Pacific Avenue). The latest evening fashions. [Courtesy of The Museum of Art & History@The McPherson Center, Santa Cruz, California]

1924–Miss California Comes To The Boardwalk

Fred Swanton convinced the Chamber of Commerce to sponsor a Miss California Pageant to draw publicity to the city. Some local citizens were outraged at "the indecency of girls wearing too much makeup and showing too much skin."[67] Nevertheless, 2,000 people jammed the ballroom at the St. George Hotel on June 8, 1924 to watch Faye Lamphier crowned as the first Miss California. She became Miss America in 1925. Designed to compete against East Coast resorts, Swanton heavily promoted the event with a huge parade and caravan of beauties to the Court of the Blossoms, constructed by volunteers at Laurel and Pacific, with 50,000 gladioli planted around a pond of water lilies. Annette Kellerman and other luminaries served as judges. The Miss California pageant went on hiatus in 1928, was revived in 1933, and ran for 50 years before feminist protesters forced a move to San Diego in 1985.

The Miss California campaign prompted a concerted effort among neighboring cities to attract tourists, arguing that everyone would win if more people visited the area. Nineteen-twenty-four also marked the official opening of the four-lane concrete Watsonville-Santa Cruz County highway. On June 11 some 250 city boosters in 50 cars decorated with banners and flags made official visits to Watsonville, Salinas, San Juan, Hollister, Gilroy, and San Jose. The group started with a parade down Pacific Avenue led by the beach band, Mayor Kratzenstein, Fred Howe (parade marshal), and Samuel Leask, Jr., chairman of the advertising committee. At each site there were fireworks, a local parade, handbills distributed, speeches by dignitaries and, of course, press coverage. The day of the tour several cars got lost, there was a head-on collision, and two press cars ran off the road to avoid an accident. Two "service cars" accompanied the group to help motorists. Never a dull moment!

Plate 130 ~ 1924 First annual Miss California Pageant. Contestants on the beach at the Boardwalk. Each of the women have the name of the city they are presenting across the front of their bathing suits. [Courtesy of Covello and Covello Collection]

Plate 131 ~ Miss California beauty pageant drew large crowds in 1940. [Courtesy of University of California Santa Cruz Special Collections Library]

A similar event was planned for late August 1921 when the so-called "Glenwood Highway" (now Highway 17) was upgraded. It was never held due to the untimely death of one of the highway's greatest supporters, Santa Cruz Supervisor James A. Harvey. On August 28, 1921 at least 20,000 people drove south on the highway, as counted by people in Los Gatos.

Plate 132 ~ Santa Cruz High School swimmers, 1920. Back row, L to R: Leo Harris, Robert Howe, Coach Leland "Lee" Lancaster, Jack Aydelotte, Lawrence Ebert. Left middle row: Clark Bachelder. Right middle row: Donald "Buzz" Lent. Lower row, L to R: Clarence Royse, Eddie Frank, Seleck Miller, Donald Dakan, Laurence Canfield (later a Boardwalk president), J.W. Dickenson Curio Store on the Electric Pier is in the background. Harold J. van Gorder's sister Ethel worked at the store renting Japanese colorful tissue beach umbrellas and selling souvenirs. Hot air balloons were lofted to the right of this picture, Fourth of July fireworks from the pier were managed by Jack Werner. [Courtesy of the Harold J. van Gorder Collection]

A portion of the Pacific Fleet anchored off Santa Cruz as part of their annual visit to Pacific Coast cities. The battleship *Mississippi*, commanded by Captain P. Symington, and the *Idaho*, commanded by Captain Charles L. Hussey or Captain J.R. Pringle (the *Santa Cruz Evening News* listed both in different articles), and six destroyers visited. The *Mississippi* launched a naval balloon to attract attention but, even without that advertising, hundreds of locals visited the ships and sailors were warmly welcomed in town. The Chamber of Commerce sponsored a trip for 500 sailors to see the Big Trees, and citizens volunteered their automobiles to drive the servicemen. Ocean swimming and beach running races between the Red Cross swimming team and the sailors were arranged, the *Mississippi's* band entertained ashore on a specially built stage in front of the Casino, and half-price tickets were available to all sailors. Some of the officers dined at the Casa del Rey for lunch and the downtown St. George Hotel hosted a dinner dance. *"The boys of the fleet showed that they enjoy the good things ashore as well as on the briny, as was shown by the way they flocked into the Boardwalk dance. They were never short of partners and enjoyed the rhythmic music to the uttermost."* [68]

The following weekend featured a special exhibition boxing match, an *"exact duplication of the big prize. Two well-known experts with the gloves will take the part of Dempsey and Carpentier and so far as the press dispatches go will give a direct counterpart of the scrap blow for blow."* [69]

That summer Charles E. Canfield proposed that the City build concessions stalls from the municipal pier to the Casino buildings, and lease them during the summer to raise funds for the City (and replace the merchant's business tax). There is no indication that this ever was carried out.

For Sale Again

After a successful 1921 summer, October brought ominous changes for the Boardwalk. On October 18, 1921, the *Santa Cruz Evening News* reported that private negotiations, initiated by Southern Pacific Company (which owned much of the Casa del Rey), were underway to sell the Santa Cruz Seaside Company and Casa del Rey properties to a group headed by John Tait. That group also owned a hotel in Paso Robles. Tait confirmed there were discussions but "no deal yet" and that "no structural changes at the beach are proposed at present, but there will be a general brightening up of the properties in line for next season's business." *"Santa Cruz has been living somewhat on the glory of its past and we propose to advertise what we shall have to offer visitors at the beach. Santa Cruz should know how valuable the new state highway is to the town, enabling the run by automobile to be made from San Francisco in less than three hours. Had this road not been completed this purchase never would have been entered upon."* [70] Tait wouldn't reveal details but local stockholders told the *News* that they would net "comfortable" profits. The *News* also reported that there were approximately 7,000 shares of stock in the Seaside Company, with S.W. Coleman owning more than 50 percent. San Francisco's J.D. Grant and the Hotaling Company were other large shareholders. Locally F.W. Howe, W.S. Moore, Samuel Leask, R.L. Cardiff, J.W. Dickinson, A.O. Goldstein, J.R. Williamson, Robert Farr, Mr. Smith, and Whitney Brothers Company, among others, were stockholders.

Recalling an earlier 1911 law suit, ownership of an entire stretch of sand between Westbrook and Main streets with a width of 90 feet south from the esplanade (some of the area between the Casino and the Municipal Wharf) was once again in dispute between the City and the Union Traction Company and

Mrs. Minnie E. Hihn, Fred D. Hihn, and Mrs. Agnes Hihn Younger. The California State Supreme Court eventually ruled in favor of the Hihn family this time.

Police Chief F. Hannah appealed to the City Council for help with pedestrian and traffic safety issues, especially between the St. James Hotel and the Casino, sparking discussion about ways to better control traffic. The community also wanted to make the winter season attractive to visitors so that facilities and businesses could be utilized year-round. The Seaside Company decided to experiment by keeping the Casa del Rey open all year. In October they featured a Halloween dinner dance at $2.00 a person. Publicity cards were handed out to summer Boardwalk visitors telling them of the great winter season plans and inviting them to return later in the year.

Also that fall, the Navy arrived to help celebrate Roosevelt's birthday which had been designated national "Navy Day." The battleship *New York* and eight submarines based in San Pedro, with their supply ship, anchored offshore. Some of the submarines were opened to visitors, a Navy baseball team challenged all comers, officers made themselves available for speeches at service clubs, and fireworks lit the sky at night. Captain A. Bronson was in charge of the flotilla.

The Restroom Dispute

The City Council complained privately, then publicly, that the Seaside Company wasn't providing enough restrooms for the public, especially for women and children. Most restrooms were inside "for pay" facilities. The Company agreed to develop a plan to improve conveniences and instruct beach attendants to admit women and children to the restrooms. When things didn't improve, the City Attorney, George W. Smith, was asked to research title to properties on the beach, including those held by the Seaside Company, hoping that the City would have more say in regulations, including providing comfort stations. Smith reported back to the City Council that his study of titles showed that the land from the middle of the Casino building to the Municipal Pier belonged to the City, but apparently nothing came of this until later.

Boardwalk officials began lobbying City Council members. A tour by City officials found 34 unlocked toilets (nineteen in Cottage City, one at the Scenic Railway, one at the hippodrome, two at the hot baths, three near the grill, two off the ballroom, one near the main entrance, and four in the emergency medical facility). Officials said the problem was caused by the fact that visitors congregated around the main entrances and the bandstand. Mr. Royce indicated that he didn't think the City could take any legal action against the company. The Mayor backed off some but said that, *"up to a certain point the company can go as far as it likes, but not when the situation becomes a detriment to the City. Unfavorable advertising concerning the locked toilets is now spreading over the state and it is bad for both the City and the company."* [71]

The Santa Cruz Federation of Parent-Teacher clubs sent a letter to the City Council on July 23 complaining about the locked toilets, saying that only four of the 34 unlocked toilets were actually available to children (you had to be a paying customer to use the others). Commissioner Royse said he had discussed the matter with R.L. Cardiff of the Seaside Company, who had made an offer to remove the locks on the condition that the city compensate them for the water used and the services of matrons. The city declined and the issue was never resolved.

In February 1921 the "whip" ride was replaced by a big new concession called "Dodge 'Em." This ride had been popular on the east coast and the Seaside Company hoped to duplicate its success here. *"The pleasure seekers ride in small electric vehicles in a large space, the little cars running around in such as fashion as to just avoid collisions and cause all kinds of excitement. An area on the Boardwalk measuring 42 x 90 feet, where The Whip concession was last year, will be utilized for the new joy makers. The cash outlay will amount to about $20,000."* [72]

A.O. Goldstein reported in April that he would be installing a "latest wonder of science" radio telephone service in his ice cream concession at the beach. April also saw Commissioner Fred C. Royse working with the Southern Pacific Company to improve safety in the Boardwalk area, and with others to create more parking spaces at the end of Beach Street near the river.

By 1922, the heavy summer season began as early as April, which saw extremely heavy traffic. By noon parking spaces at the Boardwalk were full. The Chamber of Commerce reported the July 4, 1922 weekend saw the largest crowds in history. A large number of visitors brought camping equipment because most rooms were full. Local campgrounds were all full and the *News* reported that "thousands" of autos lined every street.

George Puckett of Puckett's College of Dancing in San Francisco was one of those visitors and said the Casino ballroom was "absolutely the best appointed place and had the best floor of any dancing stadium west of Chicago."[73] The Casino started mid-week dances beginning with a barn dance. *"The Casino will be fixed up like a country barn and participants are asked to put on their oldest clothes, the girls to be in ginghams or anything suitable for the occasion. Prizes will be given for the best makeups."* [74]

July 13, 1922 saw a water wedding at the Boardwalk. *"The Principals will be rowed out to the raft and don their clothes which will be out there, jump into the water and there the ceremony will take place."*[75]

At about this same time Cardiff confirmed rumors that he was trying again to sell the company.

That summer, the Casino became a sound stage. *"Moving Pictures will actually be made. Local talent in the cast...the first opportunity ever offered to see yourself in pictures. Admission 25 and 50 cents."*[76] Santa Cruz also joined a national advertising campaign run by California, Inc., a publicity firm. The organization printed brochures, supplied feature articles, and even had movie shorts promoting central and northern California attractions.

Increased traffic brought increased risk. Five year-old Neil Fanoe of Gonzales was injured when he fell from the seat of the Scenic Railway while it was moving. He was dragged a short distance and sustained a broken hip and badly injured his right calf. Mr. Brown, manager of the Scenic Railway, quickly took him for medical attention.

Full page summer weekly newspaper ads in 1922 highlighted the many things to do at the Boardwalk:[77]

"1. *Supplying the Inner Man – ice cream and soft drinks in the parlor overlooking the bay... a comfortable place for rest and refreshments. Main rotunda of the Casino.*

2. *A memento of Santa Cruz – a souvenir handkerchief embroidered with name or initials. Novel things in leather, aluminum, and glassware. As you enter the main Casino door – the first concession to your right.*

3. *Drop Your Pennies where they give you the most fun. Penny Arcade. Main floor of Casino.*

4. *Different Taste for Sweet Teeth – Flo and Martie's Pure Candies. On the Boardwalk near main beach entrance to Casino.*

5. *They're Irresistible! Hot Dogs and Beck Beer at the Beer Garden on the Boardwalk. Dancing day and night.*

6. *Beach Front Treatments. Massage, Internal Baths, Hot Salt Baths, Feet Treated. Mary Jane Hanly, experienced nurse, Boardwalk. Phone 353.*

7. *Watch Lemos at His Painting. He does his canvasses while all who care to may look on. Wander through his art display and choose an attractive picture to send home. Main center of lower floor of the Casino.*

8. *Casino Ball Room, Regularly Weekly Double Dance – Ball Room and Grill. Midweek Special Dance: '49 Camp, Get Your Whiskers Ready. Roulette wheel, faro bank, crap tables, and all the furnishings of an old-time gambling hall will decorate the Casino while the costumes are cowboys, cowgirls, miners, dance hall girls, Chinamen, Indians, typical gambler…*

9. *The Best of Dance Music, fine orchestra, every evening during season, 6:30 to midnight. Casino Grill, Alexander Bros.*

10. *Sam's Square Deal Concession. Puritan Hams, M.J.B. Coffee, Silverware, Lamps, Alive Red and Yellow Head Talking Parrots. A full line of attractive designs in table lamps, portieres, Sheffield silverware, and novel panel-shaped self-heating percolators. Puritan hams with the taste so different and plenty of sugar, coffee and olives. At the Lotto Booth you will find these special large boxes of Baums assorted chocolate. Remember a camera for your vacation memories is waiting for you at the album and camera booth.*

11. *Delicious Coffee and Waffles. 25 cents. Waffle parlors on the Boardwalk in the Natatorium building.*

12. *Speed Boat Trips 50 cents. The last word in thrills, in refreshing pleasure, in excitement. Aqua-planing, 50 cents. Regular launch rides 25 cents. Boats from Casino pier.*

13. *Bang!!! Down go the clay pipes. Shooting gallery joys at the beach. Prizes for good marksmanship are offered daily. Keep your hand in while on vacation. On the Boardwalk, Natatorium building.*

14. *Crispettes. Not the teeth-breaking kind – but the best that are made on the Pacific Coast. Buttered popcorn, peanuts, and other goodies at the Pop Corn Stand, Boardwalk near the main Casino entrance.*

15. *Found!!! In the Casino at the beach, a wonderful place to eat with a wide variety of choice foods to select from, changed daily. Popular prices. Come and eat with us at the Cafeteria. Joe J. Smith, Mgr.*

16. *Beach Chairs! Umbrellas! All the comforts of the hours spent on the sands. Tuck the family under one of our big sun foolers. Curio store, main floor of Casino.*

17. *Can you bowl at Santa Cruz as well as at home? Try it in the alleys on the Boardwalk, near the scenic railway. See what you can make. J.P. Denney, Prop.*

18. *Launch Trips Over the Bay. The most delightful ride imaginable. Big launches, expert boatmen. Leave the Casino pier every few minutes. Look back on the beach from the bay. 25 cents.*

19. *Eat when you like, what you like, all you like. Casino Cafeteria, two entrances – main floor of Casino and Beach Street. Strictly popular prices. Everything in season.*

20. *All the World's News and the best literature printed in magazine form can be obtained at the Casino News Stand. Read while you spend your vacation on the beach. We also carry a full line of Bathing Suits and toilet articles. Main floor Casino building.*

21. *Beer on Draught. Just what you want these hot days. Hot dogs and Sauerkraut – the kind that drives away that empty feeling after swimming. Dancing day and night. Beer Garden on the Boardwalk next to the bowling alley.*

22. *Ladies attention! Visit the fancy needlework concession and look over the many beautiful things on display, including table covers, neckwear, silk hosiery and many articles of underwear. Tell your friends about it. The Fancy Good Concession. Located on the Boardwalk next to Photo Gallery."*

Ralph Miller, superintendent of the Natatorium was interviewed that summer and asked about how swimming had changed. *"The bathing dress of a young lady, thirty or forty years ago, came below the knees and had sleeves that reached to the wrist. This outfit was completed with stockings, a cap and a straw hat. Often a pair of gloves and a mask for the face were used to prevent sunburn. This is quite different from the young flapper of today with her one-piece bathing suit and her desire to acquire a slick coat of tan."* Miller relates how gasps of horror and astonishment greeted Miss Alice Boston of Santa Cruz, who was the first girl to appear on the beach without the customary stockings. The shock was so great that a criticism of her daring action appeared in the Santa Cruz newspapers.

In those days it was a common event for swimmers to swim to the whistling buoy and back. The distance was 1 5/8-mile from the old railroad wharf which was located west of the present municipal pier. Boats accompanied the swimmers but assistance was never required. *"Mr. Miller states that no one has ever been drowned while swimming at the Santa Cruz beach. Well-known people of those days, who often made the swim, were Miss Carrie Swank, who is now in the Santa Cruz post office. Miss Swank was presented with a gold ring on July 4th 35 years ago, after swimming to the buoy and back in record time."* [78]

There were many regular swimmers at the beach, including Louis Schoenberg of San Francisco who had come to the beach annually for 50 years. *"It was interesting to hear that when he first came here apple trees grew on Pacific Avenue. Mr. Schoenberg was one of Mr. Miller's first patrons when the latter opened the Neptune*

Bath House on June 20, 1883. Mr. Schoenberg goes in the water rain or shine and finds it beneficial to him." [79]

The Giant Dipper

In October 1923, Walter Looff of Long Beach (son of Charles Looff) and Manager R.L. Cardiff began negotiations for construction of a new $50,000 ride to replace the Scenic Railway. In January 1924 Arthur Looff was granted a building permit for the Giant Dipper roller-coaster.

Looff had been designing coasters along the west coast. He tried to create a ride that had "the thrill of a plunge down a mine shaft, a balloon ascent, a parachute jump, airplane acrobatics, a cyclone, a toboggan ride, and a ship in a storm." This was seen as another positive vote for the Chamber of Commerce plans to develop a year-round tourist season. It was built at a time when dance marathons, pole-sitting contests, and endurance stunts were all the rage. Looff joined the Chamber in May of that year and began an active participation by making a donation of $350 and buying two tickets to a big rally dinner held at the Casa de Rey. Looff also built a seven-room house in Santa Cruz to use when he visited. Dana Morgan of Morgan Manufacturing in La Selva Beach built the cars that run on the Dipper's tracks.

L.A. Thompson's Scenic Railway was taken down and Dipper construction began in the same area. Amazingly built in five months so that it could be ready for the summer season, the Dipper opened for business on May 17, 1924 when Arthur Looff and George Reid, manager, sent three trains of ten cars each heading up the wooden track. A visitor claimed, *"It looks as though the thrill of the aeroplane, the appeal of swift flight through space in an automobile, the hurry and rush of a railway train and a good many other things have been subdued into a well-ordered and controlled mechanism to give mankind all the pleasure of such travel with none of their dangers."* [80]

According to Looff, the Dipper required two big schooner cargoes of lumber, and a truck load of bolts and nails, two carloads of concrete, and a big car load of steel track. *"The roofing used to cover it would be sufficient for a building covering half a city block. The paint which covers it would be sufficient for sixty cottages."* [81]

Everyone was concerned about safety but Looff insisted that it was virtually impossible for the cars to leave the track because of the way upper and lower steel surfaces surrounded the track. A local newspaper article announcing the opening said that, *"Inspection of the minutest detail have made the structure of the giant dipper a fool- proof thing. The cars and tracks will never cause accidents to happen. As long as the passenger sits still he is all right, said Mr. Looff. When you hear of an accident on a Giant Dipper you may be sure that person who suffered it was standing up indulging a propensity to show off."* [82] Indeed Looff's statement has been prophetic. Although several deaths followed, it was bare never the integrity of the cars or track in question.

Plate 133 ~ 1920s bathing beauties showing bare legs. [Courtesy of University of California Santa Cruz Special Collections Library]

Plate 134 ~ The Giant Dipper 1924. [Courtesy of the Covello and Covello Collection]

The Dipper eventually required 327,000 feet of lumber, 743,000 nails, 24,000 bolts, and 63,000 pounds of steel track and safety iron. Lumber was provided by Homer T. Hayward Lumber, the motor by Santa Cruz Electric, concrete work was by T.F. Costello, the cars provided by Prior and Church (Venice, California), insurance by C.E. Canfield, hardware by Newhall & Little-field, and steel by Berger and Carter from San Francisco.

The first Giant Dipper death occurred four months after its opening. Fifteen-year-old high school student Walter Fernald Byrne, "one of the best liked and promising local youths," was killed in an accident September 21, 1924. Walter and friend Nome Ferguson were completing their fourth consecutive ride on the Dipper when both stood up in the front car near the end of the ride. An alert attendant, Adolph Brutt, saw Byrne fall head first out of the car onto the track. He immediately applied the emergency brake system which stopped the car within 15 feet, but Byrne had fallen under the car and had already been crushed to death.

Other fatalities occurred in 1940 and 1970. The car seats have been redesigned several times to make them more form fitting and the restraints made even more secure. Safety inspections include a walking inspection every two hours and an annual city inspection. Major repairs, such as replacement of wood and track, are completed in the winter. The Dipper is on its third set of passenger cars, but it is otherwise virtually unchanged since the day it opened in 1924. It even survived the 1989 Loma Prieta 6.9 magnitude earthquake.

Plate 135 ~ 1925 building the Giant Dipper Roller-coaster. Looking towards the San Lorenzo River mouth. [Courtesy of Covello and Covello Collection]

The Giant Dipper's design is simple. A large chain turned by a 70 hp electric motor hauls cars to the 85-foot peak. Riders first travel through a dark tunnel, then emerge into the sunshine, climbing upward with views of the bay. Gravity does the rest, whisking cars along steel rails at a top speed of 55 mph. The ride lasts about two minutes and travels less than a mile.

Over 45 million people have ridden the Dipper over the years. It is a registered historic landmark and has appeared in several movies: *The Sting II*, 1981; *Sudden Impact*, 1983; *The Lost Boys*, 1987; *My Posse Don't Do Homework*, 1994; and *Thrill*, 1996.

Today's coasters, such as the smaller Hurricane built in 1991, rely on computers and technology for operation. The Giant Dipper is still run by a human operator.

The Casino boasted a new coffee shop in 1924, replacing several other concessions. H.M. Lawrence, designer of the fixtures at the World's Fair in San Francisco, designed the kitchen and dining room. It was *"modern to the last word, artistic in appointment and under a management which will give the public something a little better than can be found at any resort dining room on the Pacific Coast."*[83] New wooden ceilings covered the former steel beams, golden drapes with old rose valances, and dark red mahogany furniture completed the upscale room. Electric equipment *"is an outstanding feature of the Coffee Shop. The customer orders a broiled fowl. It is placed in a rotisserie which keeps it revolving in a heat produced by electric current until brown and ready to serve. Perhaps the order is for waffles. Electric waffle irons turn them out, done without a turn for the iron cooks both sides at once. [A refrigeration] ammonia system has been installed throughout the entire restaurant. Even the drinking water passes through a coil of pipe which renders it ice cold without having ice added to it."*[84] Miss Bessie Jarvis was in charge of the floor operations. Waitresses were dressed in costumes, California poppy in color.

The new coffee shop opened its doors at precisely the same time the first Giant Dipper car ran. An hour later the Casino ballroom opened with the first dance session of the season. Hundreds visited the new shop the first evening and gave rave reviews. The main attraction of the evening, of course, was the new ride that generated "mirth, laughter, and shouts of enjoyment." One man called it "a combination of a bucking bronco, an earthquake, a whirlwind, and Niagara Falls." A local businessman was quoted, "Mr. Looff has provided an attraction which will bring thousands to this beach."[85]

Fred Swanton announced that his West Cliff housing development, which had failed, was now to be turned into an airport. About 600 feet of frontage on Cliff Drive two city blocks (1/2 mile west of Ocean Cliffs and between Sacramento and San Jose streets) was to be the official Santa Cruz landing place for aircraft of all kind. Initially there were no buildings, only a wind sock to show the direction of the ground wind.

Plane Scare

Also that summer, Pathe cameramen were on the beach filming for their newsreels. *"Scenes featuring Pilot Holloway in his seaplane in which Miss Phillipa Parker stood on its bow in midair doing stunts while Henry Josephs, skipper of the power yacht Edith S., performed on the tail, were taken as were also pictures of the latter riding waves on his surfboard accompanied by Miss Ella Stringham. The three famous McAlpine swimming school juveniles, Dorothy Lou Smith, aged five, Nadine Lyons, aged seven, and young Miss Gribble, aged seven, were photographed by Pathe while swimming from shore to the end of the Pleasure Pier."* [86]

Plate 136 ~ A seaplane took tourists for short sightseeing trips. The plane later crashed and further flights were cancelled. [Courtesy of the Harold J. van Gorder Collection]

A major airplane incident took place in 1924 when a seaplane carrying passengers crashed into the water. Bennie Throp, publicity manager for the

Boardwalk and Miss Lilla Rita Gallaway of Sacramento were on the plane with pilot H.H. Hollaway who was doing his normal plane rides for visitors. At 2:15 p.m., while performing stunts, the engine apparently quit. Because the plane was so low it dove straight into the water about 50 yards from shore, about 75 yards east of the Pleasure Pier. Thousands on the beach and at the Boardwalk saw the accident. Pilot Hollaway went into the water before the plane hit and was only slightly injured. People on a nearby speed boat jumped into the water to help Thorp and Gallaway who were trapped under the water, still in the plane. Both were rescued but Thorp had very serious, potentially fatal, injuries. Gallaway was treated and released.

In 1924 the Seaside Company acquired seven acres of John Leibbrandt's estate property near the mouth of the river, where today there is a parking lot. The intention was to spend over $300,000 on a seawall and dredging to permit boats into the San Lorenzo River, and create new amusements and bathing areas. Crowding was always problem during the summer and the Seaside Company saw expansion as a way to spread out the crowds.

Weekly summer advertisements give a good picture of the 1924 Boardwalk attractions: [87]

"1. *Refreshments for Boardwalkers at the Beer Garden next to the Giant Dipper. Free Dancing.*

2. *California's Fascinating Ice Cream Parlor. Overlooking the beach, main Casino building. Soft drinks and fancy ice cream dishes and refreshment novelties of all kinds. Goldstein Brothers.*

3. *You want a Garage Near the Beach. Storage, oils, gas, first class repair work and accessories. Beach Garage opposite Casa del Rey.*

4. *Flomart, Inc. at the beach where finest candies are sold at prices which are most inviting.*

5. *Monterey Bay Fish. Caught by our own boats and sold at right prices. Wide variety and absolutely fresh – nothing better in California. Foot of Pacific Ave near Municipal Pier. Phone 415. S. Faraola's Fish Market.*

6. *You Think You Have Had Thrills but you'll never know the real thing 'till you ride the Giant Dipper.*

7. *The Ideal Fish Restaurant, at approach to the Municipal Pier.*

8. *Baseball Sunday. Memorial Park grounds. Santa Cruz vs. Ignatians of San Francisco. Laurel and Blackburn Sts. Admission 35 cents and 50 cents.*

9. *Down Here To Tone Up Your Worn Out Body? Call on Mary Jane Hanly for massage or baths or other treatment. Get well with her help. Hanly Massage and Chiropody Parlors. Casino. Phone 353.*

10. *Modern Service Finest Cuisine St. Francis Grill. Opposite children's playground. Popular Beach front restaurant. Short orders, steaks, chops, oysters. Fish dinners. Family trade solicited. For reservations phone 370.*

11. *More for your money at any one of Sam's Concessions.*

12. *Lounging on the Beach Sands is never so perfect as when enjoyed under one of our 'big top' umbrellas. Casino Curio Store, main Casino building. J. W. Dickinson "Rent 'em or buy 'em."*

13. *California's Leading Resort Restaurant is The Coffee Shop (main Casino floor). Right prices, efficient service, delightful surroundings, metropolitan variety in menu. Short orders or an elaborate dinner – and good coffee always.*

14. *Indian Dance August 13th 8:30 p.m.. Prizes given for the best make-up as an Indian, squaw, brave, either comical or serious. The Indian ensemble "Navajo" [will play]"*

In the fall of 1924, the Santa Cruz County Fair was held for the first time at the Boardwalk. Utilizing the beach and adjoining areas, two mammoth stock tents were raised. The flagship Seattle visited Santa Cruz for three days, coinciding with the fair.

In the spring of 1925, waters at the mouth of the San Lorenzo River were placed under health quarantine by the State Board of Health due to sewage contamination from 17 septic tanks that emptied into the river. False rumors quickly spread that the Plunge water was contaminated and Boardwalk officials scrambled to assure visitors that the Plunge itself was fine. They emphasized that their own private filtering system eliminated any potential problems with ocean water. Obviously they were also concerned about the overall effect on tourism. The City struggled with how to correct the problem for at least another year.

The St. Francis Grill, facing the Casino on the northerly side of the esplanade, had stayed open all winter and, according to Peter Pappas, proprietor, had a steady flow of visitors. A.O. Goldstein of the Casino "Refreshtaurant" installed new "Ice-ci-cle" machines at 10 locations for visitors. Nineteen-twenty-five also saw an extensive line of "up to date" beach chairs along with the rental umbrellas. Summer visitors had the regular special Wednesday fun night dance plus Friday and Saturday night dances which now had two orchestras playing simultaneously – one in the main ballroom and another in the grill room rotunda. Obviously dancing was popular!

That summer's advertisements for Boardwalk attractions included:[88]

"•   *Fish dripping from the sea. Poultry, nothing more tender or served in more sanitary fashion. Chickens, ducklings, fry rabbits, squabs. "Once a customer, always a friend."*

•   *Goebel's at the Wharf. Phone 48.*

•   *Beach comfort under one of our big umbrellas. Big curio store, main Casino floor.*

•   *A full meal 25 cents including Sauerkraut, two rolls and potato salad at the Beer Garden on the Boardwalk near the Giant Dipper.*

•   *Give us the care of your automobile while you're here. Complete service. Storage, washing, repairs, supplies, oil and gas. Crankcase flushing, oiling and greasing. Beach Garage opposite Casa del Rey.*

•   *You don't know the best cooking in Santa Cruz until you've dined at the St. Francis Grill on Beach St. near the Casino – in sight of the ocean waves.*

•   *The restaurant that's different. Tell them you had dinner over the breakers. Ideal Fish Dinners. Ideal fish restaurant. Approach to Municipal Pier. Open 8 a.m. to 8 p.m.*

•   *On with the Dance. Kramer and His Jazz Boys. Casino Ballroom. Every night but Sunday.*

•   *The biggest kick at the beach – a ride on the Giant Dipper*

•   *Eat high-grade candies at the Bingo Game on the Boardwalk. Free seats. Sam, the ham man. Puritan.*

•   *Yep! It's a refreshtaurant. The place where nearly everybody at the beach takes a little refreshment or eats a dainty lunch. The most sightly eating place in the Casino. Main Rotunda overlooking the sands.*

•   *Ride with Kelso. The careful aviator. Look down on Santa Cruz pleasure land from your sky seat. $2.50 a ride. Flying field on West Cliff Drive, near Swanton Beach Park.*

•   *Flomart. Where everybody buys candy. Most for your money. Located inside of Casino on Boardwalk in front of bandstand and in Hippodrome building.*

•   *Tastiest confection on the Boardwalk. Salt water taffy. 5 cents to 50 cents. Made fresh all the time at our stand near the Palace of Fun. Victor Marini. Seven Boardwalk Stands.*

•   *A weekly "change costume" dance where girls appear as boys and their boyfriends as girls.*

- *Go fishing with Bill Johnson on the Bay. Boats leave landing on Municipal Wharf approach daily at 7:30, 9:00, 10:30 a.m. returning at 9:30, 11:00 a.m. and 2 p.m. Fare includes lines and bait $1.50. Ladies and gentlemen accommodated."*

Pilot Floyd Kelso negotiated a deal for exclusive control of the Swanton "airport" to run his sightseeing business, a flight school, and "long distance" passenger flying. In July he started special "smoke screen" flights over the beach by the Boardwalk, and on Saturday nights he did an illuminated night flight with a brightly lit plane and a double tail of fire trailing behind.

There was a special three-day Labor Day celebration in September. It was also announced that the Hihn family, who had succeeded in their court fight to own beachfront property, were now selling the site to the Seaside Company for approximately $60,000. The property was bounded by Main, First, Westbrook, and the bay. Shortly afterwards the Seaside Company announced they would build 40 "Spanish Type" two- and three-story apartments on the lot with two interior courts.

San Lorenzo River Area

Bertram B. Snyder chaired a community forum in January 1926 to talk about extending the Boardwalk from the west side of the San Lorenzo River from Kay to Water streets. Two hundred people attended and "heartily endorsed" the plans. The Seaside Company would extend their present walk about 2,400 feet around the bend and along the river bank as far as Kay Street. They intended to add a water attraction with chutes nearby, and possibly others later.

George P. Becknell told the crowd that, *"The San Lorenzo as it courses through the center of the City could and should be made the most beautiful attraction in Santa Cruz...the building of a river Boardwalk will do more towards making this city a year-round resort than any other one improvement...No matter what else may be said, our biggest income is from our visitors and whether we admit it or not, we are in the show business. We have to present the new and different or our supporters will tire of us. Our Boardwalk project has been flashed far and wide over the state and people are now saying 'the old town is waking up.'"* [89]

A.O. Goldstein explained that rights of way had been granted by property owners for the entire length, hoping that it would increase the value of their property. H.R. Judah, Jr. suggested that the $35-40,000 construction cost could be paid by local banks issuing notes, with interest, and local businessmen buying the notes. F.M. Garrison argued that it should be paid for by a city tax because the entire city would benefit, and then R.L. Cardiff suggested that various organizations could sponsor sections and get recognition through plaques. Mrs. Fred McPherson, Mrs. Alice Dixon, and Mrs. Hazael Marsh Piper then spoke up endorsing the idea but Mrs. Piper asked about the unsightly backs of buildings facing the river. Leslie Crenbourne said that the "City will undoubtedly adopt a proper zoning law." Care was taken by several officials to point out that none of the work could take place until the sewage problem was permanently resolved. The Seaside Company began work on their portion July 15, 1926.

Pappas Bathhouse Controversy

Controversy spilled over into public view in May 1926. The Seaside Company had long wanted to control all of the real estate in the area so they could provide uniform development (and, of course, make more money). Other citizens thought the City was already too lenient with the Seaside Company and should provide more direction. This became very public on May 13 when Peter Pappas, beach restaurant owner, tried to get a city permit for a new bathhouse, accommodating 1,500 people a day, on the beach front across the esplanade from the foot of Westbrook Street. The single-story stucco building was to be about 50 x 90 feet with dressing rooms in the back and glass windows facing the ocean. Mr. Pappas planned an admission price of $.25 for adults and $.10 for children (less than the Boardwalk Plunge).

Mayor W.O. Kerrick said he was strongly opposed to any more construction in the area for esthetic reasons. Pappas said that he knew that Robert Cardiff was trying to get the City to condemn all of the private property parallel to the esplanade as a way of gaining control of the area. *"The Casino runs 75 feet onto City property on which no taxes are paid, why don't you condemn that?....The City spent $10,000 putting up a fish restaurant for private parties on the beach on City land and cuts off the entire view of the cliffs, but I can't put up my own bathhouse on my own property...The trouble with me on the beach is that ice cream sodas have been reduced from 25 cents to 15 cents and that hot dogs have been brought to a price that people can afford. Who did all that? Peter Pappas did it. If the Beach Company wants this property it can afford to buy it. The City shouldn't buy it and give it to the Beach Company."* [90] The permit discussion was tabled for a later meeting.

In June, Waldo Coleman held a public meeting at which he announced the Seaside Company was preparing to issue 2,000 more preferred shares of stock to the public to "permit the further development of the beach properties." Four dollars annual dividends were offered on the $50 shares. Payment terms were made available. *Mr. Coleman said that he and his associates believed that such a property as the Seaside Company owns and manages at the Santa Cruz beach should rest as far as possible in the ownership of all people. It might not be practical to have such a property controlled by a municipality, but the nearest approach to municipal control would be such a community ownership as would be represented in the holding of stock in the enterprise by the largest possible number of citizens."* [91]

Mayor Kerrick said he *"favored the improvements of the esplanade and the keeping of the beach from the municipal pier to the Casino as a public playground. He said we must be careful not to make the mistake here that was made by Long Beach in permitting beach ground to be taken up with buildings. Long Beach, he added, has since realized its error and is buying back the beach lands so as to throw them open again to the public."* [92]

Mr. Coleman added that "the Seaside Company was essentially a local institution and that eleven of its fifteen directors were Santa Cruz men." Financial figures showed gross earnings of $199,429, with operating expenses and taxes $151,467, giving a net operating profit of $47,962. Depreciation of $23,100 lowered the net profit to $24,861. [93] [Of course other companies and individuals having businesses at the Boardwalk brought the total profit for the entire operation much higher.] October 24 saw a large ad in the local newspapers formally offering the stock for "public spirited citizens who are interested in the development of their community." [94] Some saw it as a power move against the city.

Meanwhile, 800 Democrats descended on the Boardwalk for their 1926 summer convention, and Sam "the Ham Man" Haberman moved his businesses closer to the Pleasure Pier (he had been on the other side of the Plunge) supplementing his ham and bacon business with bingo games and a new shawl and pillow concession.

The Fourth of July week saw the usual flurry of activities including the P.A.A. Championship [women's] swimming races; Miss Gertrude Lake singing songs at the Bandstand; a special "kiddies" day with beach activities; the *U.S.S. New Mexico* arrived in the bay, welcomed with a special "naval costume dance;" arrival of yachts from San Francisco; Santa Cruz Golf Club Tournament; *U.S.S. New Mexico* Band; dinner dance for officers at the Casa del Rey; dance aboard the Casino yacht in honor of officers and their ladies; entertainment by the "Woodcraft Boy Indians;" yacht races in the bay; John Philpott's ten-piece

Midshipmen Orchestra performing; Captain Leahy and officers entertaining leading Santa Cruz citizens and ladies at tea aboard the *U.S.S. New Mexico*; and topped with Fourth of July fireworks and special dancing.

City Commissioner Uriah M. Thompson noted at an August meeting that Mary Jane Hanly, who operated a Casino emergency hospital in conjunction with her Hanly Institute massage and salt bath parlors opposite Pleasure Pier, be compensated by the City for her work. She had served hundreds of injured people without any return. Some wondered why the Seaside Company couldn't provide the compensation. The Mayor said he would investigate. Two months later it was announced that Hanly had leased the Seaside Company hot salt tub bathing establishment for the next year and she intended to keep it open year round. Apparently she continued to provide first aid services as part of the deal.

The Seaside Company felt the need to publish a "correction to rumor" stating that, *"The band concerts now being held at the beach every Sunday throughout the summer season are being paid for entirely by the Santa Cruz Seaside Company, and not by the Chamber of Commerce. This applies to the summer season only."* [95]

Nineteen-twenty-six also saw the Santa Cruz Kennel Show with over 300 canines at the Casa del Rey hotel tennis courts. The Casa del Rey announced that they would remain open until November 6 instead of all winter as the previous year.

Samuel Leask's Seaside Store on Pacific Avenue advertised "Bathing Suits that Swimmers Wear" in a large *News* display. *"The most important thing about these suits is their outstanding worth. They are knitted of the finest long fiber virgin wool worsted. Like a fine silk stocking, their style is in their fit and the style lasts as long as the suit – which is a long, long time. The colors include the new stripes and jacquard effects, as well as the conventional shades…Jantzen $6.75; Cadets Jantzen Suit $5.50; Wil-Wite $7.50; Gantner & Mattern $3.75 to $8.50, cotton bathing suits $1.65 to $1.95.*[96]

In September 1926 S. Waldo Coleman confirmed rumors that the company was purchasing all of the Southern Pacific land in the Boardwalk area, which it had previously leased, at a price around $150,000.

On New Year's Day, 1927, the Seaside Company invited people to dance at the newly named "Dreamland" room in the Casino Ballroom. *"The dancing will continue from nine till one.…[with] big surprises and enjoyment.……Perfect order is the aim of the management and courtesy to its patrons is the watchword of this well regulated institution …we will do our best to please you with snappy music, fast numbers, latest song hit choruses and everything that goes to make a really first class dance. Frank Macauley, manager."* [97]

Freak Storm

In February 1927 a freak storm whipped the California coast causing extensive damage locally in Capitola, Seacliff, Seabright, and at the Boardwalk, as well as along West Cliff Drive. Half of the new seawall at Swanton Beach was destroyed by breakers. The "al fresco" stage attached to the land end of Pleasure Pier and the main bandstand on the beach in front of the Casino rotunda both collapsed and were destroyed.

George Goebel's fish and poultry market was extensively damaged, including his brand new refrigeration system. The entire esplanade between the pier and the Casino building was gone, and telephone wires dangled from their poles. The *Evening News* reported that "all storm loss is uninsured coming under the classification: an act of God."[98] The rain-swollen San Lorenzo River flooded the entire lower city area with two feet of water. Many buildings were destroyed as the water flowed freely through the city.

S.W. Coleman announced two weeks later that the company would immediately start construction of a new seawall and esplanade, including repaving the street, but he expected the City to contribute the public share. Pleasure Pier was strengthened with additional piles and stronger guard rails.

Santa Cruz invited newsreel camera crews to the Boardwalk in late April so they could film a preview of the annual May 1 pole dance performed by 36 local girls, who followed the event by a dip in the ocean. Miss Dorothy Wing directed. The hugely popular film was shown in many theaters, including New York.

Peter Pappas finally won his battle with the City Council in 1927. They rezoned the property (90 feet wide) directly opposite his St. Francis Grill restaurant to "business" which allowed him to build his bathhouse there. It was labeled in the newspaper as a compromise although there was nothing noted about what Pappas had given up.

Plate 137 ~ 1927 storm. [Courtesy of The Museum of Art & History@The McPherson Center, Santa Cruz, California]

Plate 138 ~ High tides destroy the Bandstand. [Courtesy of the Harold J. van Gorder Collection]

Plate 139 ~ Beach area wave damage. [Courtesy of the Harold van Gorder collection]

A month later it was disclosed that the Seaside Company had purchased all of the Pappas properties in the area (bounded by First, Cliff, and Westbrook and reaching to a point on the sands nearly 90 feet south from the esplanade – excepting only properties owned by George Wilkes and Ralph Miller) for $150,000. Pappas retained the right to operate his restaurant for an additional two years. *"Mr. Coleman said that one of the principal reasons back of yesterday's sale was to assure without doubt a beach front clear of structures of an undesirable type for all time. As a result of the deal the structures on the beach erected by Mr. Pappas opposite his restaurant will be taken down and the proposed bathhouse project… will not be erected."*[99] Coleman also tried to push the City Council into beginning promised work to repave Beach Street. After weeks of delay they finally agreed to issue the contract but the Southern Pacific Railroad immediately filed a serious lawsuit declaring that their portion of the expenses was unjust.

Coleman relocated all of the picnic tables at the foot of Westbrook Street to the end of the Boardwalk near the San Lorenzo River and created a picnic area there. Locals applauded both the new scenic area and the reduction of "clutter" in the wharf/beachfront area. A caretaker's building and concessions for hot dogs, coffee, and ice cream were created. The entire area was free, safe, and popular with parents and children. The Seaside Company also received kudos for continued cleanup of the area between the Casino and the wharf, including the addition of a "natty awning" over beach chairs for use of Casa del Rey residents. The Giant Dipper continued to draw crowds to the lower end of the Boardwalk.

Santa Cruz Is Backwards, Low Class, Drab and Overcharges

City officials continually battled public perception that Santa Cruz was "old news." At a 1927 Rotary meeting, R.L. Cardiff said that it was time to realize that Santa Cruz *"presents a drab appearance, that its summer patronage is not all that it might be, that many summer visitors are overcharged for rooms"* – and that something needed to be done. He hired the Johnson-Ayres Advertising Corporation to send out 4,000 questionnaires to companies and individuals within a 250-mile radius of San Francisco. Hundreds more were personally interviewed. *"The majority of these persons stated that between the mountains and the seashore they preferred beach localities for spending of a vacation. Of all vacation sports they preferred swimming…A number of persons interviewed in this survey declared frankly and emphatically they had given up coming to Santa Cruz because of its drab appearance, class of summer patronage and over charging…the report states that we can never expect to draw the Del Monte patronage though there is no excuse for us to have the 'Coney Island' crowd. It names the respectable middle class of ranchers, business men, and retired persons as the ideal Santa Cruz vacationist and prospective settler."* [100]

Johnson-Ayres also found that Santa Cruz people were equally negative. *"The latter declare that the prices we charge summer boarders are sure criminal and that this is a city that depends on summer trade and is sure a dead one during the winter… The report tells us frankly that we are a very old, backward city and that only when all civic organizations and every other interest in the community gets together can we open things up and present a modern, impressive appearance."* Rotarian H.R. Judah concluded that, *"This is a condition we have to meet right now…People come here for a good time and expect to find the accompanying aesthetic surroundings."* [101] Mr. Judah referred to the esplanade's condition as a typical civic eyesore.

Few disagreed with the findings and it became a mayorial campaign issue. In May Fred W. Swanton was elected mayor in a landslide victory. Part of his platform was to "zoom ahead resort-wise, civic-wise, and industrially." [102]

Hot weather drove crowds to the Boardwalk that summer, and two submarines and two Coast Guard cutters parked in the bay helped draw crowds. Traffic to the area was high and many noticed the increased number of automobiles parked everywhere in the area.

And then there were the trained fleas. At Professor Ruhl's Flea Circus concession, *"By the aid of magnifying glasses, the fleas can be seen drawing a cannon, a chariot and carriage. The fleas have also been trained to jump through hoops, dance in costume and operate a merry-go-round.* "[103]

20th Anniversary

June 1927 featured a special 20th anniversary dance and celebration at the Casino, celebrating the second reopening after the devastating fire. In retrospect it had been a very full and exciting 20 years and the slogan "Never a Dull Moment" couldn't have been more accurate. A Lantern Carnival program was arranged with *"thousands of colored lanterns hung from above the Boardwalk, the Casino, the Pleasure Pier, and all the concessions will make the scene a mass of light. The carnival will be opened at 7:30 p.m. by an illuminated Boardwalk parade led by a giant dragon 60 feet long carrying…bathing girls and led by two knights in armor."* [104] Entertainment at the Bandstand followed. Later in the week there were fireworks displays on Pleasure Pier, a circus parade on the Boardwalk with elephants, bulls and matadors, and a speed boat race.

M.C. Hall, publicity director for the Seaside Company for the past two years announced he was leaving for a position at the Del Monte Hotel. Alvin K. Matthews, former editor of the *Santa Cruz Morning Sentinel*, replaced him.

The Seaside Company announced earnings from August 1, 1926-July 31, 1927: Gross earnings $191,030; Expenses, $147,803; giving a net operating profit of $43,227. Other income of $2,648 and interest paid of $12,606 gave a net profit of $33,260. Dividends to stockholders equaled $23,151 or about $100 per stockholder.

Paving around the Boardwalk finally started in 1928. The area in front of Cottage City and Casa del Rey apartments was completed in early spring, bringing the first paved thoroughfare to the beach. The boardwalk was extended along the San Lorenzo River and a new river bathhouse was added with complete facilities to assist visitors with both surf and river swimming. An open-air dance pavilion, a new miniature railway, and a "chute the chutes" ride were added to the attractions. Dancing at the Boardwalk was 20 cents a couple, which paid for 1-15 hours (!).

In February 1928 the Seaside Company held their annual public meeting. S. Waldo Coleman, opened the meeting with a speech saying that, *"Community development should be owned by citizens of Santa Cruz…and the most practical way for the people of Santa Cruz to own beach property and aid in its development [was] for them to use the group that had already been formed – the Santa Cruz Seaside Company."* [105] For the first time the internal organization of the Seaside Company was disclosed to the public. Comptroller M.L. Smith oversaw day-to-day operational matters. Fred K. MacDonald handled all of the Casa del Rey hotel operations. Alvin K. Matthews, Events Manager, handled conventions, exhibits, sports, dances, and general entertainment. Vice President R.L. Cardiff provided day-to-day executive oversight.

In his speech, Coleman pointed out that in 1927 the Seaside Company had received 63,858 newspaper columns of free publicity, the number of stockholders had increased from 164 to 288, they had purchased the Pappas and Southern Pacific properties, 46 new rooms had been added to the hotel, the Casino building was renamed to Beach Auditorium, and river front facilities were added. It was quite a year!

Plate 140 ~ 93 year old J.B. Jarrett, Miss 1928 Martha Friede and Mayor Fred Swanton at the New Year's Flower Show, 1928. [Courtesy of University of California Santa Cruz Special Collections Library]

New directors were elected: R.L. Cardiff, S. Waldo Coleman, F. R. Howe, William T. Jeter, Walker W. Kamm, C.J. Klein, Samuel Leask, F.A. Zane, F.I. McCaffrey, W.L. Moore, W.S. Moore, George A. Montell, J.A. Pilkington, Lester Wessendorf, and J.R. Williamson. Fred MacDonald resigned his position in May and moved to Texas along with his wife. Pat O'Connor, former manager of the Appleton Hotel in Watsonville, was hired to replace him.

A new miniature railroad, designed and operated by Stanley E. Kohl, was finished in late March. The route was nearly a mile in length, included an engine car powered by gasoline, a box car, passenger cars, and an observation car. It ran through a tunnel under the Boardwalk near the Dodge 'Em ride.

Southern Pacific continued to provide special visitor trains from San Francisco on Saturdays and Sundays. It was a two-hour, 40-minute trip from San Francisco and increasing numbers of people came for the day.

Spanish Gardens

The highlight of the 1928 season was the official opening of the Casa del Rey Spanish Gardens on March 31. A large part of the Cottage City was torn down to free up land that was planted with a variety of plants and trees, and a glass solarium and children's playground were added. The *Santa Cruz News* claimed that several early visitors had proclaimed it the best garden in the west. Royal purple petunias, red and purple tulips, strawberry plants, rhododendrons, and 200 rose bushes complimented a green lawn with gravel paths. A sundial from Spain and French café iron tables and chairs were placed around the garden for tea service and afternoon refreshments. Entrances to the gardens were built from Dolphin Street, the hotel lobby, and the tennis courts.

Mrs. Elizabeth Burbank, widow of Luther Burbank, donated a walnut shade tree to the gardens. A letter from Luther Burbank dated January 16, 1926 read, *"You will have no trouble in helping to beautify Santa Cruz for it has a better climate for growing plants than any place without exception in California. I know what I speak of because I have visited the place and spent much time there during the past fifty years."* It took six months, 43 workmen, nine gardeners, 1,500 loads of soil, 300 pounds of grass seed, 3,000 plants and shrubs, 3,000 feet of irrigation piping, and "several thousands of dollars" to complete. Many local Santa Cruz firms provided expert help but the majority of the garden work was done by Seaside Company employees to save money.[106]

In May Carl Harris announced the opening of the Ham Tree Restaurant at 154 Beach Street. *"Specializing in baked hams, fried chicken, southern style and the famous Jambo Negg sandwich (of which we are the inventors). Home made pies, cakes, biscuits. Two famous cooks: Bernice Harris and Rose Gilbert."* [107]

There was also discussion with the City and property owners about improving the lighting on Beach Street from Pacific Avenue to the river mouth.

On June 22 S. Waldo Coleman voluntarily resigned from the presidency of the Seaside Company. Robert L. Cardiff, manager of the Coast Counties Gas and Electric Company, was elected in his place.

The *U.S.S. Maryland*, one of the largest fighting ships at the time, docked off Santa Cruz that summer and stayed through the July Fourth holiday weekend. The usual dances, parades, visits to the ship, and concerts followed.

With the increasing number of visitors, the Boardwalk saw an increase in the number of minor crimes and in July the Seaside Company asked the City to provide a policeman at the beach. *"The company pays approximately $15,000 annually in taxes and part of this naturally goes for police and fire protection...[we are asking] for protection of the thousands of visitors as well as local people who visit the beach and Boardwalk. You will agree with me that during the summer months and especially over weekends there are thousands of people at the beach and in fact on some occasions there are more visitors to Santa Cruz than the entire population of this city. Naturally criminals make it a point to mingle with large gatherings and it is for the protection of the public that prompts me to ask that the City provide a police officer in uniform."* [108]

Beach Ownership Dispute – Again

The City Council and Mayor Fred Swanton held conversations in July with Alvin Matthews of the Seaside Company about finally settling the issue of which beach property belonged to the City. The City's position was that the ground occupied by the lower rotunda, by the entrance to the auditorium, was on City land, along with the Pleasure Pier and a triangular area connecting the pier and the Boardwalk where vendors sold goods to the public. The City believed that people renting the bandstand on the beach, as well as vendor stands on the beach near the river, should pay monies to the City. One beach area was actually fenced off for a vendor. Swanton reminded people that part of the Beach Auditorium and Boardwalk were also on City property. The Seaside Company countered that they cleaned the beach regularly, had paid for part of the paving of Beach Street, paid city property and utility taxes, and had recently started paying for lighting. Vendors had City licenses and the City should deal with them, not the Company. The City announced their intention to file a legal suit asking for back rent and Mayor Swanton threatened that, "It would not be a friendly suit."[109]

The same day the City held a surprise health inspection of all the Boardwalk vendors, the Seaside Company and the Casa del Rey. Some saw the timing as a subtle threat about the power of the City over the Seaside Company.

At the end of 1928, two days before Christmas, R.W. Mariland Jr. of Oakland made an emergency landing on the hard sand at the Santa Cruz beach, scattering a few dozen people who were on the beach at the time. He landed his gray biplane successfully, turned around, and parked near the Hippodrome. *"Hot Dog Miller, the beach concessionaire, served the aviator with several of his famous hot dogs to assuage the appetites of the two travelers."* [110]

Plate 141 ~ Beach fashions. Date unknown. Three boys on the right have swim suits that say "Neptune" on the front. Pleasure Pier is in the background. [Courtesy of University of California Santa Cruz Special Collections Library]

After the 1929 summer season, renovations to the Casa del Rey began converting 120 rooms on the third floor into 45 three-room housekeeping apartment units. Hamilton and Church did the construction work and the first six units were completed in December.

Val C. Waterman and Mrs. Alma O. Muth, owners of the Ideal Fish Restaurant, purchased the adjoining Sylvester Fish Restaurant and then joined the two buildings into a larger unit.

The end of the 1920s brought more changes to the Boardwalk. The roller skating fad was waning nationally, but it continued to thrive in Santa Cruz. In 1929 Roy Hammond was appointed the first roller skating rink manager. He was a commercial artist in Santa Cruz and a former skating partner with Harley Davidson. A 10-piece brass band played from a platform hung from the rafters while skaters circled below on the maple hardwood floor. The rink was closed after three years, the fad finally having run its course.

Plate 142 ~ Santa Cruz resident Lilis Teshara with an unidentified friend. On the Boardwalk in front of the kewpie doll concession, early 1920s. [Courtesy of University of California Santa Cruz Special Collections Library]

The Meese-Godfrey company was awarded a $6,000 contract to install new water chutes machinery at the mouth of the San Lorenzo River in May 1929. Stanley E. Kohn managed the project. The chutes were twice as high as the previous ones. Approximately 360 feet long, three "boats" were pulled by an endless cable to about 85 feet and then plunged down the track at 60 mph until they hit the bottom water with a big splash. A large 40 x 18-foot concrete tank captured sea water and then used it to move the boats.

Plate 143 ~ Inside the roller rink. Probably about 1908. [Courtesy of University of California Santa Cruz Special Collections Library]

Robert L. Cardiff was re-elected president of the Santa Cruz Seaside Company at the annual meeting in 1930 along with Fred R. Howe, vice president, Laurence Canfield, secretary-treasurer, and H.L. Cunningham, assistant secretary-treasurer. A total of 13,360 shares were outstanding as of the March 1 meeting. Hugo Norbeck, former manager of the Casa del Rey from 1920-28, returned to the Seaside Company as an assistant to Cardiff.

More Legal Battles

Attorneys Everywhere

In April 1930 the City of Santa Cruz and the Seaside Company appeared to settle their long running battle for title to property at the beach, under legal pressure from the city. The City agreed to deed the Seaside Company the land occupied by part of the Beach Auditorium and the bath house, and in return the Seaside Company agreed to relinquish any legal title to all other beach land, all the way to the San Lorenzo River. Both sides began preparing the required paperwork for court approval, but a month later a legal title expert hired by the Seaside Company, Henry E. Monroe, issued an opinion that the City did not in fact own the land. Based on the original City incorporation grant, surveyors' field notes from 1858-9, and California state law, Monroe's opinion was that the City owned land only to the high tide mark, and the state owned land from there into the bay. Some locals thought that because the public had used the beach land continually since earliest memories that this established rights to the City, but Monroe disagreed.

In retaliation twelve days later the City approved John Tait's San Francisco construction company plans for a large amusement center at the beach. The plans called for spending $500,000 on *"a two-story semi-circular building covering approximately 280 feet frontage along the esplanade in front of the Municipal Wharf. The west end of a Beach Auditorium will extend fifty feet beyond the wharf and is to run parallel to the esplanade. In this section will be a penny arcade. Behind the arcade and running 250 feet from the wharf's northern end will be a fish restaurant. On the eastern side of the wharf will be a dance pavilion behind ice cream parlors. Next to the parlors will be the concessions and the extreme eastern end will house a plunge and locker rooms for men and women. The building is to be of Spanish architecture with openings on the wharf. Over the main entrance to the building is to be a 132 foot tower."* [111] The City planned to lease the center to a newly formed Santa Cruz Amusement Company. Many noted that it sounded amazingly similar to the existing Seaside Company properties and obviously was intended as a direct threat to them.

On May 14 the City filed condemnation proceedings directed against the Seaside Company. City Attorney John H. Leonard stated that the City would not take any actions that would interfere with current operations of the Seaside Company until the suit was settled; the City merely wanted to ensure the beach property remained public forever. There was some concern that if they lost the suit the City would be liable for damages so the City put a $1 deposit for each of the people named in the suit on deposit with the court. Leonard said he didn't think a jury would award any more than that because the City's intent was pure and in the public interest.

On July 28, Malio Stagnaro and Luis Beverino sent a letter to the City Council stating their interest in leasing the Pleasure Pier. Most people thought it belonged to the Seaside Company but actually they had leased it from the City for 25 years, and their lease expired April 20, 1929. No one had taken any actions after the lease expired. The City immediately entered into discussions with the two men, putting more pressure on the Seaside Company. The Company responded with front page newspaper interviews that it was totally opposed to the City using Pleasure Pier and they would fight it with legal action if necessary. Mayor Swanton gave a statement at the next city council meeting that the lease had, in fact, expired and in his opinion the City could realize $10-12,000 annually from concession leases. Swanton asked the council: "Shall we advertise for bids on a new franchise or operate it by the City?" The next day Cardiff issued a statement: "The threat is part of a premeditated effort on the part of the Mayor of Santa Cruz to harass the Seaside Company." He again reminded the public that possible "large" damages would be awarded if the City lost the suit and that "the Company will use every method possible to keep the beach clear and to keep it from being built up with shacks and concessions."[112]

The City also reached a separate agreement with John H. Leonard and S. Koll, owners of the miniature railroad at the beach, who agreed to pay a "nominal sum" indicating "his recognition that the City claims title to that part of the beach which constitutes his right of way."[113]

On August 7 the courts formally directed the Seaside Company to reply to the City condemnation proceedings. The City had delayed this step until the end of summer in an agreement with the Seaside Company so that no summer activities would be negatively impacted.

Trying to sway public opinion and add additional pressure, the City began to argue in the newspapers that it had the right to eminent domain proceedings, regardless of how the title suit turned out.

Meanwhile crowds continued to flood the Boardwalk area, oblivious to the behind-the-scenes legal maneuvering. On July 29, 1930, the *Santa Cruz Evening News* reported that 16,000 people had been at the beach over the weekend. Southern Pacific ran special trains from San Francisco and San Jose, and local roads were clogged Sunday from 10 a.m. to 8:30 at night. The Boardwalk featured accordion music by locals Mario Toccolini and David Ferrari. In September it was announced that over 1,000,000 people had visited Santa Cruz during the four summer months with peak attendance in July and August.

Plate 144 ~ Aerial view of the Boardwalk area with summer beach crowds. Taken in the 1930s. [Courtesy of The Museum of Art & History@The McPherson Center, Santa Cruz, California]

More Troubles For The Seaside Company

At the end of the 1930 summer, it was announced that the Casa del Rey would not be open for the winter season due to the lack of enough reservations. Local newspaper editorials voiced the community fears that winter visitors would now go to Monterey because Santa Cruz lacked a high-end hotel. The gloomy financial situation was furthered when it was revealed that the properties had already been listed for sale with local realtor Andy Balich. In December, El Paso millionaire Harry L. Hussemann viewed the various properties and met with management officials. Husseman already owned property on Beach Hill and in the area of the current Pacific Garden Mall.

In 1931 the owner of the Palomar Hotel, H.C. Rohlfs, negotiated a short-term lease for the Casa del Rey with an option to buy for an estimated $250,000, and in an interview with the *Santa Cruz Evening News*, it confirmed that all of the Seaside Company properties were available for purchase for approximately

$1,000,000. Discussions continued with the Seaside Company with not only Rohlfs but also investors from outside the area.

Plate 145 ~ Summer crowds, date unknown. [Courtesy of The Museum of Art & History@The McPherson Center, Santa Cruz, California]

The February 1931 annual meeting re-elected Cardiff as head of the Seaside Company, along with Fred Howe, vice president, Laurence Canfield, secretary, and Herbert Cunningham, assistant secretary and treasurer. Cardiff, J. R. Williamson, and Laurence Canfield were also elected to head the Casa del Rey. Directors elected were A.O. Goldstein, J.R. Williamson, Lester H. Wessendorf, W. Grant Hatch, J. Ross Whiting, W.L. Moore, W.S. Moore, George A. Montell, Charles J. Klein, and Samuel Leask, Sr. None of the financials or plans discussed were revealed to the public, provoking more rumors about another business failure.

In May Superior Court Judge Harry Lucas ruled that the City of Santa Cruz had no legal right to lease Pleasure Pier businesses, saying that the beach belonged to the State. The City had already granted a lease to John Tait for the pier but William Johnson, Jr. protested, saying that, if allowed, Tait would no longer permit him to use the wharf to load people for his speed boat and fishing boat businesses. In his view, Lucas said that the wharf clearly belonged to the State of California which had granted the City ownership of the pier but only as trustee for the people to insure the right to public use.

Plate 146 ~ Boardwalk beach area, that's a children's slide towards the right. 1920s. [Courtesy of The Museum of Art & History@The McPherson Center, Santa Cruz, California]

In September the Seaside Company filed a "quiet title" suit asking the Superior Court for immediate clarification of titles for the entire beach area. This led to speculation that a deal was in the works and that the Seaside Company needed to ensure title to proceed with the sale. Named in the suit were all the people involved in the past 35 years with various property transactions in the area. Several weeks before the Chamber of Commerce had approached the Mayor and Cardiff about dismissing the various legal suits and negotiating a settlement privately, but they failed. Seaside Company attorneys once again publicly raised the threat of "damages that city residents might have to pay" and "we will never give up rights to beach land we already possess." Mayor Swanton issued a statement after the latest legal round that he would "never sign any portion of the beach over to anyone until an agreement is signed to preserve the entire sands for the public." [114]

Plate 147 ~ Casa del Rey apartments late 1920s. [Courtesy of University of California Santa Cruz Special Collections Library]

Troyer Brothers Get Casa Del Rey

On February 2, 1932, Cardiff confirmed that yet another party was interested in the Casa del Rey: three brothers from Hollywood (J. Vance, Gifford L. Troyer, and W.C. Troyer). The brothers leased the Casa del Rey, the Bay View supper room in the rotunda (the former grill room), and the dance hall in the Beach Auditorium for the summer with a 10-year renewal option, plus an option to purchase the hotel. Financial details were not announced. The brothers were especially interested in improving the restaurant, keeping the hotel open year-round, and adding another restaurant upstairs that could be rented out for special occasions. They told the press that they would be improving the covered arch from the hotel to the Beach Auditorium by covering it with flowering vines. The new arch plans were drawn up by the designer of the garden court of Hollywood's Grauman's Chinese Theater. The brothers were actively involved in day-to-day management and were popular with locals.

At the end of February 1932 the self-perpetuating Seaside Company directors were all re-elected at the annual meeting. With respect to the future outlook the only public comment was, "satisfaction expressed with prospects... all dividends were paid on preferred stock."[115]

Two wealthy investors, Alex Nibley of Los Angeles and Leonard Jones of San Antonio, Texas, visited the Seaside Company properties in March, and had initial discussions with Balich about a purchase. Unfortunately, the story leaked to the newspapers but neither Cardiff nor Chairman James R. Williamson were aware of it, and so told the *Santa Cruz News* reporter. The Troyer Brothers then became concerned that their lease might be in jeopardy. The outcome was not reported in later newspapers but the Troyers continued to prosper with the business.

On May 14 an official re-opening party was held with Carlton Kelsey's Hollywood Dance Orchestra directed by William Sodeburg. Walter Zwahlen, formerly of the Santa Barbara Biltmore, Roosevelt Hotel in Hollywood, and the Waldorf-Astoria in New York was brought in as head chef. Several businesses ran ads in the newspaper thanking the Troyers for their efforts. Paul Fairchild, distributor of soda, ginger ale, lemonade, umbrellas, and "aids to entertainment" wrote, "Let's all back the Troyer Brothers... All money spent in this town is good for your business and mine... the greatest thing since Marion Hollins came to town is the new leadership of the Troyers." [116]

Two-piece Bathing Costumes

In April 1932 the City Council took on more important matters than land titles. Gantner and Mattern, San Francisco manufacturers of bathing suits, announced they were putting on an exhibition for council members at the court-house lawn so they could look at new two-piece bathing "costumes" proposed for the beach front. "These garments have been considered legal on many beaches because they do away with the practice of 'rolling down' the other type of bathing suit, which makes for vulgar exposure," remarked the manufacturer's representative.

The *Santa Cruz News* included a large publicity picture of the two-piece suits on its April 22 front page. The swell of public interest caused the organizers to move the event to the beach to accommodate expected larger crowds. Four newsreel companies and a radio station announced they were covering the event, and asked the City for policemen and a paddy wagon to be "ready for any flagrant violations of whatever law it is that has to do with daring swim suits." They made sure the newspaper reported that fact which drew even larger crowds. Then the organizers said they needed 13 additional young models and asked local women to audition at the Hotel Palomar.

Don Patterson and several lifeguards volunteered to be present at the beach in case any of the women required rescuing. The mayor and four commissioners did their public duty and witnessed the event before a crowd of 4,000 locals. After an hour of examination of 27 beach suits, Mayor Swanton asked the crowd for their reaction and received back popular approval. Orville Webster Jr., former superintendent of the Christian Church Sunday School, couldn't understand why there should not be some cloth attachment between the trunks and the brassieres of the women's suits. There were few remarks when nine male models showed off their new one-piece suits. Exhausted, the Council retired to their chambers to begin drafting a law "dictating what will constitute modesty for Santa Cruz beach this summer." [117]

When the fun was over, City Commissioners Orville Webster Jr. and Noel Patterson reported that they had met privately, at the Mayor's direction, with Seaside Company officials yet another time to discuss the legal matters about property ownership but had been "unable to get the representatives of the company to come to any agreement with us…This is what the City has found in all of its experiences with the Seaside Company." Mayor Swanton told the press that, "It's got to come to a show down…I don't want to hurt the Seaside

Company, but I don't want the City to be hurt either." The council decided to continue with their legal condemnation proceedings.[118]

Plate 148 ~ Officials examining bathing suits for modesty. Fred Swanton (right end of the table), Orville Webster, Police Officer Doyle and city officials carefully examine proposed 1932 bathing suits to make sure they are sufficiently modest. [Courtesy of University of California Santa Cruz Special Collections Library]

Eliminating Sin

On the heels of the two-piece bathing suit revue, some local residents began a campaign to close down all alcohol sales and gambling. These "vices" had always existed in the city and occasionally the laws were enforced, but most of the time the city had "other priorities." Local churches pushed the effort and several newspapers wrote editorials endorsing the idea. Mayor Swanton responded with a statement to the City Council saying he advocated circulating a petition to local businessmen and, if there was consensus and the City Council allocated funds for more law enforcement staff, then he would "do everything within my power" to close down the establishments starting with the beach and working up Pacific Avenue and into the rest of the city. Liquor revenues were a substantial part of the Boardwalk income.

D.L. Hughes, local pastor of the Garfield Park Christian Church, was irate and said he would never sign such a petition because the Mayor and City Council should already be enforcing the laws. J.C. Colyar, retired clergyman and prominent poultry man, added, *"Officials know that bootlegging and gambling places are running in this city, and if they don't they are not qualified as officers…Mr. Colyar went on to say that he knew personally of several 'joints' that were running, apparently unmolested, and that he and several of his friends had taken the trouble to watch the crowds that patronized gambling house in Chinatown and elsewhere. I have had complaints from several persons in the city that the Chinese are taking the business away from the whites."* [119] Eventually the issue faded away.

Boardwalk concessions saw some improvement starting with the renovation of a popular turnover pie concession stand. The Coffee Shop was gone; instead a new type of game called Uncle Fred's was operated by Fred Gross. A new auction booth was operated by Boen and Bender, a brand new Dante's Inferno dark thrill ride, the Lindy Loop, Aeroplane, and Kiddies Auto Ride now pleased the crowds. The salt water Plunge was cleaned and repainted.

The summer of 1932 saw big crowds in Santa Cruz during the Fourth of July weekend. An estimated quarter million people visited the area, including 150,000 in the Boardwalk beach area. The Suntan Special train ran from San Jose, Oakland, and San Francisco and delivered people in Santa Cruz. Typical Sundays saw 3,500 departing from the train. The Troyer Brothers said that 20,000 had stayed, visited, or eaten at the Casa del Rey during the three-day weekend, a seemingly impossible number. Boardwalk concessions reported higher than expected income. The crowd was in a spending mood despite the country's economic slump.

Former Ohio residents had a special treat when a chartered train arrived with 148 Ohio visitors to spend 24 hours visiting the area. A special dinner was held for them and locals with Ohio connections at the Casa del Rey, followed by a public show attended by an estimated 6,000 people.

November saw the first visit by a naval ship since 1929. The *U.S.S. Salt Lake City*, a 10,000-ton heavy cruiser, anchored in the bay. Sailors and officers participated in an Armistice Day parade and later celebrated at a special event at the Casa del Rey, followed by dancing at the Hula Bowl. Officials commented that despite having 500 sailors in town there was surprisingly little disturbance of any kind.

The Beach Band reformed in April 1933 with Thomas Simmons as leader. New musicians with both classical and modern jazz training were recruited for a schedule of 23 beachfront concerts in the old bandstand by the Plunge. The band hadn't performed since 1921 and they were welcomed back remembering the "good old days." The Southern Pacific Band continued their performances in the Beach Auditorium and the ever-popular Saturday night Carnival Nights were renewed at the Beach Auditorium with the Casino Rhythm Kings providing the music. Half-price days for children were put on the calendar and the maypole dances revived. On Mother's Day 150 large containers of flowers were placed on the bandstand and a free afternoon eulogy on "Mother" with a sacred concert by "electrical transcription" followed. Fifty young pupils of the Gregory Dance School also appeared.

The Troyer Brothers renewed their lease of the Casa del Rey for another three years and announced that they would be renovating most of the hotel rooms and redecorating the theater auditorium. They also considered making the Bay View dining room in the Beach Auditorium building into a beer garden.

S. Waldo Coleman returned to take a more active role in the Seaside Company. The Directorate now consisted of J.R. Williamson who was elected President, Fred R. Howe, Samuel Leask, W.L. Moore, W. Grant Hatch, W.S. Moore, Charles J. Klein, Lester Wessendorf, A.O. Goldstein, Laurence Canfield, George Montell, S. F. Gilman, H.L. Cunningham, S. Waldo Coleman, and L.J. Jenkins (from Coleman's office in San Francisco). H.L. Cunningham was designated as secretary-treasurer and A.J. Menne of San Francisco was elected assistant secretary-treasurer.

Work commenced on extending the Boardwalk around the river in April. Six men were employed to dig holes for the iron rail supports and clear away brush. Iron rails from the former chutes ride and scrap wagon rims were used to construct the eight-foot-wide pathway.

Malio Stagnaro announced that he was installing a 275-horsepower engine in the speedboat *Miss Stagnaro*, replacing the 100-horsepower engine. He also added two additional boats to his growing fleet at the Pleasure Pier concession.

In May, William Johnson, speedboat and fishing trip operator, had a 265-foot barkentine ship towed from Oakland to a point 3 ½ miles off shore, a convenient ½ mile beyond government control. Built in 1919 by George H. Hinds of the Rolph Shipping Company for sugar transportation, the ship was transformed into a "floating amusement palace." Johnson said that it could accommodate 500 fishermen, "while inside will be accommodations for 2,000 pleasure seekers, including a giant dance hall, two dining salons, 18 state rooms, and 14 double staterooms. All variety of games and other entertainment will be on tap."[120] Johnson, of course, provided the speedboats and launches to carry people from the pier to the ship, a 30-minute trip.

In June, Arthur Looff announced that he had sold the Giant Dipper to the Seaside Company because he wanted to consolidate all of his business activity in Long Beach. The price was not announced. A wholly-owned subsidiary company, the Santa Cruz Giant Dipper Company, was created.

Over the 1933 July Fourth weekend, the Southern Pacific Band returned to give two concerts, along with a bathing revue on a specially constructed runway and stage. Ten local girls were selected to wear the season's latest designs.

The owner of the Ideal Fish Restaurant disclosed that he was reviving plans to build on the beachfront property adjacent to the wharf. He had held plans in abeyance during the City-Seaside Company land ownership disputes, but now looked for three tenants willing to sign five-year leases. He owned property 196 feet eastward from the entrance to the wharf, with an average depth of 90 feet from the esplanade railing to the high-water mark. He indicated that he was willing to sell to the City if they wanted to prevent unsightly buildings in the area and Fred Swanton supported the idea, but a deal was never reached.

"Hot Dog Miller" opened a new beer garden on Beach Street across from the Boardwalk. Miller's Beer Garden had two rooms, one facing Leibbrandt Avenue, which seated 25, and a larger lunch room for 70. The second floor was used for office space. Mr. Miller announced that he would specialize in cold Rainier and Acme beer.

Micky Malto

That summer Micky Malto came to the Boardwalk. Micky was the mascot for a new malted milk drink fad that was sweeping the country. Ralph Sooy, sales manager of the Micky Malto Products Company, worked with E.O. Goldstein, beach concessionaire, to designate a special "Micky Malto" day at the Boardwalk. More than 1,000 local youngsters paraded, a special dance by five costumed girls from the Fort-Barka School of Dancing ("the Dance of Micky Malto") aroused the crowd, and, of course, Micky appeared to help sell specially priced drinks (five cents a glass, half price). Micky Malto Kats (small figures that always landed on their feet when thrown) were given away to Santa Cruz youngsters along with Micky balloons. Sooy told locals that, *"A duty that any parent owes his child is to feed the youngster the foods that will tend to conserve the energy of the youngsters. Children use up a tremendous amount of energy in their daily play, and if the food they eat does not contain strength-giving qualities, their bodies do not grow properly... As malt sugar is the major sugar ingredient in the Micky Malto, it can easily be seen that a Mickey Malto supplies about the very best food qualities that anyone — youngster or oldster can consume.*" [121]

In the fall of 1933, Casa del Rey announced it was renovating the building to encourage locals to take up full time residence in the hotel around the first of the year. A $15,000 steam heating plant was built by the Pittsburg Water Heater Company and the local Coast Counties Gas and Electric Company to make the units "fully modern." Units from studios to four-room apartments now offered gas ranges, "steam heat in every room and instantaneous hot water at all times"... and the price included "everything but the maid." [122] Mr. and Mrs. John A. Poschmann continued as resident managers.

The Seaside Company repainted the Giant Dipper and reupholstered the cars, moved the entrance, and strengthened the support structure. The wooden boardwalk from the Beach Auditorium to the Giant Dipper was surfaced with 11,000 square feet of Calrock, reducing complaints about splinters and women's narrow heels sticking between the boards. A new "drive-ur-self" ride opened with gasoline-powered automobiles which ran on a track.

Before the 1934 season began the Casino ballroom was renamed the Cocoanut Grove ballroom.

E.J. Reicher put up a new building opposite Pleasure Pier that housed a concession named "Life" which came from the Chicago World's Fair; Nathan's Barbaquette Inn was a new concession in the Plunge building, operated by Nathan Aboudara, offering barbequed foods, sandwiches, and beer. The Plunge was repainted and renovated, and a new pricing policy went into effect that offered reduced rates if customers provided their own swimming suits, and two free days for children when the Plunge first opened. A new attraction, the "Four Jacks," featured trapeze acrobatic acts 200 feet above the beach in front of the Fun House.

Crowds were thick in the spring of 1934 and local businessmen were optimistic that two years of upgrades were beginning to pay off. Twenty thousand visitors thronged to the beach and Boardwalk the first weekend in May and 1,200 Saturday night dancers exceeded attendance for the past five years. The July Fourth weekend saw crowds twice that size due to an additional 12,000 who attended the Portuguese Holy Ghost festival.

Plate 149 ~ Auto Speedway concession about 1930. [Courtesy of University of California Santa Cruz Special Collections Library]

Over Labor Day weekend there were special swimming exhibitions including Don Patterson's amazing "fire dive" in the Plunge, and Sylvest, the strongest man in the world, driving spikes with his bare hands and lifting four men at once. Seventy thousand visitors crowded into Santa Cruz, delighting local businessmen. Ten thousand people crowded the beach to view Jack Carney's Hollywood Steppers and over-capacity crowds of 1,500 danced at the Beach Auditorium. All hotels were full that season and parking was at a premium.

The summer seasons were lasting longer each year. Admissions Day weekend saw a new "slide for life, featuring a daring lady aerialist, Mademoiselle Vernabele, hanging by her teeth while she swirls dizzily down a tight wire from the lofty Beach Auditorium tower to the end of the Pleasure Pier over the bay waters."[123] The San Francisco Dolphin Club announced that their champion swimmers would compete in the first annual Santa Cruz ocean race from the Fun House, about half a mile out in the ocean, around a buoy, and then back to the Plunge building. The Beach Band presented two free concerts and the Gregory Dancing Kiddies appeared in a free revue on the open-air stage, followed by a special farewell to the season program by the Beach Auditorium Carnival Club in the Plunge.

In September the Casa del Rey announced a new lower price structure for winter rentals, once again positioning themselves to keep the place open year-round.

After serving as secretary-treasurer of the Santa Cruz Seaside Company since 1929, Herbert L. Cunningham resigned and was replaced by Charles G. Howell, son-in-law of Dr. W. Grant Hatch, a Seaside Company director. Mr. Cunningham also purchased a Photo-Strip concession and equipment for a Boardwalk store plus the "Pig Game" opposite the Pleasure Pier.

At the end of the year, two famous dance orchestras played at the Cocoanut Grove during the holiday season: The Jay Whidden Orchestra, featured in 50 movies at the time and well-known throughout the country, along with the Lenny Rapose Orchestra featuring Miss Emily Carlyle. The Troyer Brothers also brought in the comedy team Kolb and Dill who had played at the Beach Auditorium 25 years earlier for an evening of "intimate style" theater at the Casa del Rey.

J. Ross Whiting, manager of the Giant Dipper and former chief engineer at the Casa del Rey, was promoted to general superintendent of the Seaside Company in January 1935, replacing Joseph B. Lane. Lane took over ownership of the frozen custard concession on the Boardwalk, a highly desirable business. J.R. Williamson, president of the Seaside Company, announced that a new motorboat ride at the former open-air dance platform at the lower end of the Boardwalk was being installed under management of Don Sinkinson of Santa Cruz. In a large tank, the self-powered boats carried passengers over a circular course. Also planned were a skee-ball game in the Plunge building in the space formerly occupied by Sam Haberman's ham and bacon concession, and a giant Ferris wheel. Pleasure Pier was re-decked and the piers strengthened; the Beach Auditorium roof was replaced, plants were put along the entire north side of the complex, and many of the buildings were repainted.

Seaside Company Properties Almost Profitable

At the annual Seaside Company meeting in February 1935, President Williamson was happy to announce that for the first time in many years the company was operating at a profit. Gross earnings of $120,025 and expenses of $116,342 left the company cash flow positive $3,682 but expenses of $19,800 resulted in an actual book loss of $16,177. The Giant Dipper subsidiary company generated $6,633 to the parent company. Gross earnings were not revealed but Williamson's report said that they had increased $35,453 over the previous year and that assets, including real estate, were valued at $395,726. He also announced that the company had purchased the Whip ride and the miniature train. The Board of Directors remained as: James R. Williamson, president; F.R. Howe, vice-president; Laurence Canfield; S. Waldo Coleman; C. Howell; W. Grant Hatch; L.F. Hinds; L.W. Jenkins Jr.; Charles J. Klein; Samuel Leasks, Sr.; George Montell; W. L. Moore; W.S. Moore; and Lester H. Wessendorf.

Plate 150 ~ The rebuilt casino. From a color postcard about 1909. [Courtesy of Chandra Beal]

Rumors circulated that several of the concessions recently pushed out by the Seaside Company were talking with Val and George Goebel about leasing space in their newly proposed building at the shore end of the Municipal Wharf. Waterman confirmed the discussions but said no leases had been issued. Mayor Roy Hammond reiterated that he was "flatly in opposition to any building on the beach front," which he believed to be against the wishes of the citizens. He expressed doubt, however, as to how any such move could legally be prevented.

At the same time, Southern Pacific Railway submitted plans to the City for a pedestrian "subway" under the tracks at Beach and Leibbrandt streets. The pass was described as box-type 7 x 6-foot tunnel with a siphon to carry off water. It was unclear who was going to pay for the work and the City indicated they had no funds available.

No To Raggin' In 1935

But the big news in 1935 was a new City ordinance, adopted at the urging of some local churches and the Women's Christian Temperance Union, banning "raggin" anywhere in the city. *"It shall be unlawful…for any person to dance or participate in the dancing, at any public gathering or assemblage, in the City of Santa Cruz, of any of the dances commonly known as the 'turkey trot,' 'Texas Tommy,' 'grizzly bear,' 'bunny hug,' or any other dances similar in character to said dances or any dancing known as 'raggin.'"* [124]

Violators faced a $100 fine and up to 30 days in the city jail. Fred Swanton posted signs in the Beach Auditorium: "BEWARE OF ARREST. By order of the mayor and commissioners of the City of Santa Cruz, you are subject to arrest if you dance the Rag, Turkey Trot, Texas Tommy, or other similar dances." Swanton left enforcement up to local officials. To the *Santa Cruz News* he explained that, "We will not stop anyone from dancing the Turkey Trot or any other similar dances, [125] as long as they dance them correctly." [126] In what must have been the first of its kind, "A few days later a select audience in the Beach Auditorium ballroom had the prized experience of witnessing Chief of Police Jones….demonstrate the 'decent and indecent' method of dancing." [127]

A skee-roll contest was held to introduce the new concession at the Boardwalk. Prizes included a radio, a Japanese lacquered serving table, and an electric clock. The Plunge officially opened the same day with hours 1 p.m.-10 p.m. weekdays, 10 a.m.-10 p.m. weekends. April saw two big dance orchestras at the Beach Auditorium: Scott Held's popular orchestra at the Cocoanut Grove and Anson Week's Mark Hopkins Orchestra from San Francisco in a special one-night engagement. The annual Easter Egg Hunt offered 1,000 prizes to youngsters.

A $2,500 damage suit was filed against the Casa del Rey in June by Helen E. Hallinan, wife of the well-known San Francisco attorney, Vincent Hallinan, who represented her. She said that she fell against one of the steam heating pipes in the hotel salon in May and severely burned her arm. The Seaside Company claimed it was due to her own negligence and fought the suit.

Not long after, 19 year-old Robert W. Pimtel fell from the trapeze in the Plunge and fractured his skull. He sued the Seaside Company for $50,000 but later settled out of court. Pimtel was a guest who was allowed to "try out" the trapeze.

Continuing the legal problems a $55,480 suit was filed by Roy B. Walker and Mona B. Walker against the Seaside Company for broken bones and torn ligaments that happened during a Standard Oil Company event at the Ocean Wave ride. Mr. Walker also claimed $2,500 in damages for loss of his wife's companionship during her hospitalization. She later testified at a jury trial that she "felt her foot being caught" and fell heavily, breaking her left arm. She reported that no one responded to her husband's calls to shut off the power, and that considerable difficulty was encountered in getting her out."[128] Attorneys settled the case privately before the case went to the jury.

Officials discovered that Harriett Blackburn, one of the pioneers of Santa Cruz, had earlier donated land to the City at the west end of the Beach Auditorium, directly opposite the St. Francis Grill. The Seaside Company built a children's playground on the property, with two city employees for supervision.

The 1935 Fourth of July weekend saw record crowds estimated at 100,000 in the beach area, and traffic on Highway 17 was at a complete standstill for several hours. The Seaside Company estimated 80,000 people had visited the Beach Auditorium and Boardwalk over the weekend. Four Sun-Tan Special trains carried 2,800 passengers in addition to the regular trains. Local businessmen said it was the largest crowd in recent memory and were happy at the turnaround.

In August the Troyer Brothers announced another profitable year of operation for the hotel, their fourth consecutive since taking over management. Local officials were lavish with praise for the management, reminding people that in 1934 alone the brothers had brought 10 conventions with 20,000 delegates to Santa Cruz, and that they had spent more on outside advertising than the rest of the Santa Cruz businesses combined. "Gifford L. Troyer, under whose direction the hotel's accounting department operates, pointed out that their Santa Cruz operations have been carried on in the face of the world's greatest business depression." [129]

The Clyde Diaz and Norman Handley San Francisco Olympic Club's National Comedy High Diving Team joined local Don Patterson for an evening of fun at the Plunge in August 1936, and thousands of colored balloons were set adrift on the bay near the pier where swimmers of any age could catch them and turn them in for tickets to various concessions.

In September Santa Cruz celebrated its 166th birthday with a party. The Seaside Company turned the entire Boardwalk facility over to the public with 15-cent admission for children and 25 cents for adults, entitling customers to utilize all of the Boardwalk rides.

Many Hollywood movies were shot in the Santa Cruz area during the 1930s. Claudette Colbert and Fred MacMurray stayed at the Casa del Rey during the 1936 shooting of "Maid of Salem." The *Santa Cruz Evening News* excitedly reported that they had played tennis in the late afternoon.

In October the Universal Film Company worked out an agreement with the Troyer Brothers to temporarily transform the Cocoanut Grove ballroom into a motion picture theater showing their film "My Man of Godfrey," starring William Powell and Carole Lombard, and the latest shorts. The studio used this as a vehicle to test various markets to determine whether to build permanent movie theaters. A fireproof projection room had to be built in the Beach Auditorium.

Plate 151 ~ Cocoanut Grove ballroom, probably 1937. [Courtesy of The Museum of Art & History at The McPherson Center, Santa Cruz, California]

November saw the Les Hite Cotton Club Swing Orchestra playing at the Cocoanut Grove. The band was well-known nationally and often played the same circuits as the Tommy Dorsey Band. Mae Diggs, "chosen the most beautiful colored girl in the world last year at New Orleans, will handle vocal assignments."[130]

Dance bands were always one of the most popular features of the Boardwalk and in the winter the Casa del Rey offered its own smaller events. Phil Harris and his Jack Benny Jello Orchestra played an afternoon event there in 1937, and then later at the Cocoanut Grove. Phil Harris had a regular radio program that gave him national exposure and he drew large crowds everywhere the band played. The Troyer Brothers offered "balcony loges with private tables" at the dance program.

Plate 152 ~ Children playing on the beach after Pleasure Pier was built. Signs in the background say "Electric Pier Tintype Gallery" and "Take a Ride on the Choo Choo Cars." Looks like "Gamby's Ice Cream" stand underneath the pier. [Courtesy of The Museum of Art and History at The McPherson Center, Santa Cruz, California]

At the annual 1937 Seaside Company meeting the news was good. For the 1936 season gross earnings were $215,014, operating expenses $109,605; taxes and deprecation $39,814; interest and federal taxes $23,432; for a profit of $42,160 and a dividend of $4 per share. The big increase from the previous year's profit ($12,329) was attributed by President Williamson to the concessions purchased in 1935. Williamson also announced a new concession for 1937, a giant "loop the loop." The official name was later announced as "Loop-O-Plane" and featured the equivalent of a 40-foot fall or the looping of an airplane in a dive.

J. Ross Whiting was promoted to Board Secretary and Boardwalk Plant Superintendent, succeeding Charles G. Howell, and Andrew Antonetti was promoted to Head Cashier. The Board of Directors were unanimously re-elected with: James R. Williamson, president; F.R. Howe, vice-president; Laurence Canfield; S. Waldo Coleman; C. Howell; L.F. Hinds; L.W. Jenkins Jr.; Charles J. Klein; Samuel Leasks, Sr.; George Montell; W. L. Moore; W.S. Moore; and Lester H. Wessendorf. (W. Grant Hatch apparently had resigned.) New directors T. G. McCreary, Ralph S. Miller, and Dr. L.M. Linscott were added.

The "Barbecue Inn" beach concession, in the southwest corner of the Natatorium, was sold by Nate Aboudara to Peter Warner, a new Santa Cruz resident from Minnesota.

The Cocoanut Grove reopened after renovation of the interior by San Francisco designer Marcel Rescello. Silver and white were now the operative colors, and even the palm trees flanking the orchestra stand were frosted white. A new blue ceiling was decorated with silver stars to simulate an evening sky. All the fancy plaster was removed from the stage area and white cellophane drapery served as a background for musicians. All of the 2,400 lights were removed and indirect lighting fixtures of white flashed glass were installed. The Troyer Brothers spent $6,000 on the improvements. At the same time they were working in the Casa del Rey putting stucco on the pillars, changing the ceiling color, adding new linoleum, and placing rugs in the lobby area along with massive new furniture of Spanish design.

In April 1937, Richard Albert Carona, a 16-year-old boy from Watsonville, drowned at the Plunge while taking swimming lessons as part of a 4-H event. A spectator in the gallery noticed a body underwater after other swimmers had left the children and women's pool to listen to their leader, Bob Christensen. Several Boardwalk employees tried to revive Carona and then had problems locating a doctor due to a physicians' meeting being held in Rio Del Mar at the same time.

In a September 22, 1937 speech on the 'History of Swimming' before the Women's Luncheon Club, Littlefield mentioned that there had been three drownings that year in the Plunge, after 17 years without problems.

The Plunge opened on March 21, 1938 with more renovations. The pool's sides and bottom were now painted white and water system improvements made the water safer than the local drinking water. Warren "Skip" Littlefield again directed Plunge activities (his 17th year). Stanford and San Jose swim teams competed in a water polo game, various swimming stars showed off, the two-mile swim was held again, and the summer Saturday night swim exhibition programs continued. Ruth Kahl, the Santa Cruz human submarine, traveled 303 feet, two full lengths of the huge Natatorium pool, entirely underwater without breathing.

The Standard Oil Company held a gigantic "frolic" for their 16,000 employees at the Boardwalk in mid-September. Five bands played almost continuously on Saturday. A photographer took several hundred photos of the event for a feature article in Life magazine.

October saw the start of another suit against the Seaside Company by the mother of 16-year-old Mary Alice Hawkins. She contended that Mary injured her right foot, ankle, and leg June 1, 1936 on the Giant Dipper when the cars jammed. The mother, Alleen Hawkins, was an owner of the Beach Hill Inn.

On Armistice Day, one of the largest ships afloat, the *U.S.S. Colorado*, dropped anchor off the Boardwalk on a trip to San Francisco. The *Colorado* was returning from a search for Amelia Earhart. Sailors planned shore leave with many special events, including a 'smoker' at the Cocoanut Grove, but heavy seas cancelled the shore leave after only a few sailors had made it to the city. Locals had hoped to tour the ship and watch the vessel's three planes launched via catapult. Later in the month a new submarine, the P10, visited the Municipal Wharf.

Plate 153 ~ 1950 steam train. Giant Dipper is in the background, taken from the south side of the San Lorenzo River. [Courtesy of the Harold van Gorder collection]

Over Easter weekend of 1938, Skip Littlefield arranged for another swimming training session for locals. Sponsored by Jantzen and the *Santa Cruz Evening News*, the "Learn-To-Swim-Campaign" offered six-hour swimming lessons for people of all ages as part of a safety campaign at the Plunge.

"Bosco" Patterson added a new dive in the Plunge shows, an 80-foot dive which required cutting a hole in the ceiling. The trick was to not hit the steel girders on the way down. The Troyer Brothers announced that they had leased the Casa del Rey kitchen, Trocadero Room, and Terrace Cocktail Lounge and Bar to employee Fred A. DeVaney. He promptly remodeled the kitchen, hired a new cook, and replaced all of the dishware.

Henry "Hot Dog" Miller was honored at his stand by Fred R. Howe for selling his five millionth hot dog in 31 seasons at the Boardwalk. Miller came from Germany in 1890, got a job in the first Beach Auditorium dining room and later opened the stand.

In late September 1938 a storm with a "monster ground swell" caused $1,000 worth of damage at the Boardwalk, mainly damage to pier pilings and floats. The Boardwalk was officially closed in mid-October with some concessions remaining open on weekends only. Large crowds showed up the last weekend as people enjoyed the last days of summer.

Plate 154 ~ 1938 Coconut Grove as seen from the Casa del Rey. There is still an arched passenger bridge (on the left) connecting the Beach Auditorium and the hotel. [Courtesy of Covello and Covello Collection]

Apparently, Val C. Waterman of the Ideal Fish Restaurant sold his property sometime in 1938 because on October 31, 1938, Douglas Morrison of Carmel was granted a building permit to construct a new restaurant on the property adjacent to the entrance to the wharf (the so-called Grace lots). His $6,900 budget was for a one-story frame building with 35 feet of frontage on the esplanade. It was to be "ultra modern" and "have a copper roof with a lamella design which is a semi-spherical cover so constructed as to eliminate posts or supporters within the structure."[131] He later stated it had cost $10,000 plus $25,000 for the restaurant furnishings and equipment. There was some city council opposition but most felt that he was within his rights and fighting it would be pointless. The restaurant was leased to George Jacovich of Monterey before the opening.

Repairs to the Pleasure Pier commenced in January 1939 when 40 new piles were set. The coffee shop near the Arcade was eliminated completely and the confectionary concession enlarged. The City negotiated ownership of a site at the end of Pacific Street by the wharf which they wanted for a large aquarium. A year later their interest shifted to the Lighthouse Point area as a better location for the aquarium but it was never built.

More Improvements

A large improvement program was undertaken in early 1940. The Plunge pools were retiled, and new pumps, filters, pipes, and underwater lights were installed. The entire Boardwalk underwent a spring cleaning and several smaller buildings were combined into a larger structure. Six new games were planned including the "Auto Scooter" with "modern streamlined cars faithfully reproduced in Lilliputian size" at a cost of $20,000, a $7,500 "Rollo Plane," and a $10,000 "Octopus" ride. The Casa del Rey upgraded 50 interior court rooms and enlarged the dining rooms. The Beach Auditorium was redecorated and they built a miniature ice skating rink in the center of the circular dance floor.

Williamson, Seaside Company president, stated that, "We intend to do everything within our power to build up and maintain the finest beach resort on the Pacific Coast. The history of Santa Cruz beach for the past 33 years has shown that our business has actually been confined to a three-month summer period....however, we firmly believe that with the inauguration of the new highways and the now easy accessibility to this area to metropolitan centers, Santa Cruz is destined for bigger and better business. Our organization is building for the future." [132]

Plate 155 ~ Sand castle contest. Probably 1940s photograph. [Courtesy of University of California Santa Cruz Special Collections Library]

Fred Swanton Dies

Fred Swanton died September 3, 1940 at the age of 78, just as the summer season was coming to an end. Santa Cruz's only three-time mayor, outstanding promoter of the area, and founder of the Boardwalk had been ill for several months. Although he talked capitalists into investing over $7,000,000 into Santa Cruz in various projects throughout his life, he died with very little of his own money left. His legacy of tourist trade on a mass scale has benefited Santa Cruz for nearly 100 years. Skip Littlefield described Swanton as "possessed of the imagination of a Barnum and the eloquence of a Samuel Shortridge." After his death, flags at the city hall, the courthouse, and all along the waterfront were lowered to half-mast in respect to Swanton, and he was interred at the Odd Fellows' crematory. Swanton's credo was "do it big." And indeed, he did.

Recent Times

Life went on. Advertising for the 1941 summer season started identifying the Santa Cruz beach as the "Waikiki of Western America." The first Suntan Special train of the year ran on May 18, earlier than previous years due to increased demand. Repairs on the Boardwalk under the Southern Pacific trestle at the San Lorenzo River were completed; they had been damaged in a winter storm.

The Suntan Special train trips from San Francisco and Oakland were rerouted through Watsonville instead of over the hill from Los Gatos, making the trip 20 minutes longer. Local businessmen were very concerned about this but train ticket sales were actually higher than the prior year due to extra advertising.

Reflecting the patriotic feelings of the time, Captain H. D. Swett of the 250th Coast Artillery dedicated a new steel flagpole installed at the head of Pleasure Pier by the Santa Cruz American Legion Post 64.

After Labor Day 1941, the Seaside Company added 64 more feet to Pleasure Pier to help deal with a sandbar at the end of the pier which made it difficult for boats to dock there.

Norman Wilfred "Count" Hanley led the big Plunge show in June, his third year of performing at the Boardwalk. Hanley was a comedian who spoofed swimming activities including using a rubber trapeze. Billy Rose's water ballet with a dozen mermaids was a big hit along with music provided by Maurice Kealoha and his Polynesians.

Another legal suit was filed against the Seaside Corporation by Richard Williams. He claimed his leg was broken when he collided with someone else on the wooden slide at the Fun House.

The 1941 Fourth of July weekend drew 40,000 people. A train with 10 special cars brought visitors from Chicago. Extra buses were added to bring visitors from San Francisco, Watsonville, and Salinas.

Louis Figone's 100-piece accordion band played at the bandstand, the Great Romero did a high pole act, and the Valere brothers staged a horizontal bar act. Sammy Herman's band was the evening feature. On July 9 Joe Stagnaro, known locally as the "wharf Crosby," sang his renditions of Hawaiian melodies. Two 10-year-old kids, Dick Baker and Freddie Quadros, amazed a record crowd of 1,417 people at the Plunge with a 50-foot platform dive, and Harry Kelly, also aged 10, swam the entire length of the Plunge underwater without a breath.

In August, 20-year-old Don McNair, the male "human submarine," broke the world's record for swimming underwater without breathing: 353 feet, done at the Plunge pool. He then achieved a record 405 feet underwater, three lengths of the huge Plunge swimming pool, before a crowd of 1,400 people. Ruth Kahl, Santa Cruz world record holder for women, managed 303 feet but took twice as many strokes. A total of 15 events entertained the crowd including 30 mermaids on parade in a water ballet and Bosco Patterson and his Juvenile Trapeze Stars.

Labor Day 1941 featured Mr. Chandu from Rangoon, India. The Sentinel reported that, *"He does more than eat fire. With the aid of an acetylene torch, the Mahatma finds shaving a chore of but 15 seconds. For the benefit of skeptics he will take the torch and sever a piece of iron and then proceed to throw the full force of the crackling white flame on his tongue. How does he keep from burning up? Come down and take a gander at him."* [133] Dione of the Royal Hawaiian Hotel performed "hula gymnastics," Stanley Kramer presented a well-received puppet show, and Clay Landrum played the banjo.

In August the California Highway Department released a report showing that highway traffic over the Santa Cruz-Los Gatos highway was up 13 percent over the previous July, with a total of 14,253 cars entering Santa Cruz on July 13, and about the same number of cars entering from the Watsonville direction. (There are about four times as many cars traveling Highway 17 today.)

But typical of the busy season, at least one person reported an injury. Anthony Sapunar filed a $7,400 legal suit against the Seaside Company because a carousel horse came loose while he was riding it and he was thrown to the floor, suffering several injuries.

War

In December 1941 the war effort became real locally when the Army Air Corps sounded a West Coast alert at 2:18 a.m. December 10, indicating approaching enemy aircraft. A blackout from Bakersfield to the Oregon state line was called and all radio stations were ordered off the air. Nothing happened but the city council later debated having all stores, including the Boardwalk, close at dark in order to provide protection to the city.

On December 21, the *Santa Cruz Evening News* reported that "Enemy Craft Operating Off the Coast of California Believed Suicide Effort To Hit Shipping – Tanker Flees to Refuge Here – Futile Naval Action Off Cypress Point Early Saturday Afternoon; Eight Shots-No Hits."[134] Supposedly a Japanese submarine took eight or nine shots with a deck gun at the 6,711-ton tanker the *Agriworld*, all of them missing their mark. The ship immediately fled, anchoring one mile off the Santa Cruz municipal wharf. The Navy said they could not confirm the incident but didn't deny it either. The ship's crew was not allowed off the boat and local defense officials said they hadn't visited so it is hard to know where the "facts" were coming from. Many were skeptical about the incident but rumors immediately circulated, including sightings of a periscope two hundred yards off the Twin Lakes beach.

During WWII, the Boardwalk's thousands of lights were blacked out and a curtain was put up from the Beach Auditorium to the river entrance to screen interior lights. Home Guard patrolled the beach on horseback. Tourism declined because of war rationing and the economy. The Miss California pageant and the Suntan Special were cancelled, however on Friday and Saturday nights the Coconut Grove Ballroom was still very popular.

The Plunge expected its six-millionth customer that year. General admission was now 50 cents if you needed a suit and towel, 40 cents if you provided your own suit, and 25 cents for children under 12. Leask's offered the newest men's swim trunks made of Lastex for $1.00 to $4.95 and women's Lastex colorful import prints, silk piques, and pure wool suits from $3.95-$12.95.

Homer Cornick, Superintendent of Schools in Santa Cruz, addressed the Chamber of Commerce in April 1942, suggesting that a new advertising campaign be started aimed at defense workers and those in the military. Because of the accelerated war effort many defense facilities were unable to accommodate families or even workers in some cases so many people had long commutes to work. Cornick suggested a message that men should send their wives and families to Santa Cruz for the summer, avoiding crowded and high living cost conditions in defense areas.

"A kid-created sandstorm hit an area of the beach Sunday afternoon as over a thousand kids scrambled and dug through a half-acre to find colored Easter eggs, uncovering them in frenzied activity in the postponed annual hunt of the Santa Cruz Seaside Company. To be certain of a share in the 700 eggs with their prize slips, some of the youngsters were at the beach as early as 11 a.m. to wait for four hours until the go signal. The beach saw visitors only from 3 to 6 p.m. Sunday, and speedboats were unable to operate with only 18 inches of water at the end of the Pleasure Pier because of low tides." ~ Santa Cruz Sentinel, April 14, 1942

The *Santa Cruz Sentinel* joined with the Red Cross in sponsoring swim classes at the Plunge with the line that, "It is your patriotic duty to learn to swim for health and safety." The Seaside Company pledged one day's receipts in June at the urging of the local Elks lodge to the Navy Relief Fund that helped care for wives, widows, and orphans of Navy personnel.

Plate 156 ~ Post WWII crowds waiting for the suntan special train at the Casino station. [Courtesy of the Harold J. van Gorder Collection]

Plate 157 ~ Hotel Casa del Rey – the bridge to the Casino is being demolished. 1950s? [Courtesy of University of California Santa Cruz Special Collections Library]

A new span of flying trapezes was added to the Plunge with a 35-foot tower which was used by 14-year-old prep school star Shirley Wightman and 11-year-old Freddie Quadros at the Plunge opening in June. The *Sentinel* bragged that no other swimming pool in America was so equipped with aerial aquatic rigging, and that stories about the Plunge had appeared in newspapers across America, from the *New York Times* to the *Honolulu Advertiser*. The 44th season for the Plunge showed off 50 Santa Cruz "aqua brats" from age eight and up. The featured performer was nationally known Clyde Devine, a high school coach at Sequoia High School in Redwood City, who used a trampoline installed on the 30-foot tower to perform tricks that could not be done off a springboard. Representatives from the San Francisco Olympic Club, San Francisco's North Beach pool and the Crystal Palace Baths all gave exhibitions. Twenty Santa Cruzans coached by Billie Cruse gave an aquatic ballet in the pool, performing to Polynesian music and featuring Regiment, stationed then in Soquel who dove from the 35-foot tower. Don McNair demonstrated his underwater swimming abilities and "Mighty Bosco" Patterson performed on the flying trapeze. The Plunge continued to be the focal point of the Boardwalk in 1942 with several large events planned.

In March the *Santa Cruz Sentinel* recalled one of the great swimming stars of the early days, Red Wallace, born in 1883. "He was in truth the pioneer of speed swimming, the Duke Kahanamoku and Johnny Weissmuller of post-Civil War days." Back in the "old days"[135] before ocean swimming was popular, the Soquel resident amazed locals by swimming a mile from shore and once swam from Capitola to Santa Cruz, a five-mile distance. He held the 100-yard swimming record of 59 seconds. "His swimming suit extended from ankle to Adam's apple...for freedom of action the sleeves were cut off at the elbow and when wet weighed 15 pounds."[136] At age 60 he still swam in the ocean but had given up the long ocean swims quipping that "the Coast Guard authorities might mistake him for a submarine."[137]

The Plunge changed direction in 1943, leasing the complex out to the military during the morning hours before it normally opened (10 a.m.). The Casa del Rey had been turned into a naval hospital by that time and the Plunge was used for physical therapy and to teach new sailors to swim. The facilities were also open to anyone in the armed services including young people awaiting service. Seaside Company officials said that the war effort had priority and, if needed, public hours would be further reduced in order to assist the sailors. As part of the ongoing improvements the shower rooms had been tiled in "ocean blue."

In April a new group of businessmen and politicians from Santa Cruz, Monterey, and San Benito counties met to discuss long range planning for post-war Monterey Bay. Walter J. Wilkinson, outgoing president of the Watsonville Chamber of Commerce, called the meeting and predicted that the area would see the "greatest changes in the shortest time" during the next few years. He recalled coming to Watsonville in 1900 and the way that life had changed because of the automobile. He saw similar changes coming at the end of the war and the return of some 20,000,000 people directly in the military or supporting it.

S. Waldo Coleman, Boardwalk President from 1915-1928 and principal stockholder until 1946, surprised the community by selling his interest in the Seaside Company for "in excess of $100,000" to a group of local businessmen, mostly Seaside Company directors, headed by Louis W. Jenkins. James. R. Williamson, Fred R. Howe, Lester Wessendorf, Laurence Canfield, Stanford Smith, Bert Snyder, and the Cottardo Stagnaro Fishing Corporation were involved, as well as a few unnamed smaller investors. Coleman should be credited with being a major factor in saving the Boardwalk after its first financial collapse and was widely respected in the community.

Louis W. Jenkins took over the reins after Coleman's exit in 1943 and continued on until 1951. The boardwalk began to pickup speed again after the World War II years, looking forward to the booming economy and the many new families with children and leisure time. After only a few years of leadership Jenkins died unexpectedly in 1951.

After World War II, the Boardwalk came under the primary control of the Canfield family, and it has remained under their direction ever since. It was truly the end of an era of amazing change and the Santa Cruz Boardwalk was a reflection of that change.

Laurence Canfield

Shortly after Louis Jenkin's death, Laurence Canfield, long-time Director, became President in early 1952. The Canfield family has a long history in Santa Cruz County. Dr. Colbert Austin Canfield, of Smithsonian fame, married the daughter of James Watson, an early resident who operated one of the first general stores in 1822. Charles Canfield became a grocer in 1895 and founded the C.E. Canfield and Son Insurance Company. Colbert Canfield was involved with the operation of the Dolphin Bathhouse in 1886. Caroline Mariana Canfield married David Leibbrandt, son of John Leibbrandt, in 1866.

Plate 158 ~ Laurence Canfield. Seaside Company President 1952-1984. [Courtesy of The Museum of Art & History@The McPherson Center, Santa Cruz, California]

Disneyland opened in 1955, forever changing the amusement park industry. In competition with Disney, Canfield remodeled the Beach Auditorium, planted palm trees, and installed the Wild Mouse, a high-speed thrill ride imported from Germany. The Pleasure Pier was demolished, and the Plunge was filled in and covered with a miniature golf course. Canfield removed the bridge connecting the Beach Auditorium to the Casa del Rey and a five-acre parking lot was built off Beach Street, the largest paved and illuminated parking structure in the county at the time.

Reflecting sentiments in the 1880s, Laurence Canfield said before his death, "This town doesn't understand that we're competing with every other community for the leisure dollars. A lot of people would just like the guest to mail his check over here."[138]

Plate 159 ~ Autorama at the end of the Boardwalk. Autorama was later replaced by the log ride. [Courtesy of the Harold J. van Gorder Collection]

Charles Canfield II

Charles L. Canfield was elected as sixth president of the Santa Cruz Seaside Company in 1984, following the death of his father, Laurence, and he remains in control today. Charles is a native Santa Cruzan who attended Mission Hill Junior High and Santa Cruz High School. He graduated from the University of Oregon in 1961 and saw two tours of duty with the U.S. Navy in the western Pacific. He also worked at the Boardwalk as a concessionaire in 1964.

Today the Seaside Company apparently has a five-member board of directors and about 85 stockholders. The Canfield family controls most of the stock. The Seaside Company also owns quite a bit of property in the "beach flats" area and periodically expresses interest in developing the entire area.

Plate 160 ~ Charles Canfield. Current Seaside Company President. [Courtesy of The Museum of Art & History at The McPherson Center, Santa Cruz, California]

The amusement park is generally open weekends from September through March, and daily from Memorial Day to Labor Day. A free concert series on Fridays at the bandstand continues the long tradition. Fireworks shows were stopped in 1975 "in the interest of public safety." The Beach Auditorium still stands and houses modern arcade games. The Cocoanut Grove Ballroom is used for special events. Neptune's Kingdom replaced the Natatorium. The Looff Carousel still operates and looks pretty much the same as the day it was installed. And the Giant Dipper is as popular as ever. Operating alongside the venerable classics are modern inventions, such as ATMs, hearing impaired phones, and handicapped access to the beach.

The area known as the Boardwalk has had many incarnations since Santa Cruz first put itself on the map almost 150 years ago. It has seen a long parade of colorful characters, and made and broke many local entrepreneurs. Millions of people have strolled along the promenade. Visitors who discovered the Boardwalk as children return with their own grandchildren. Each passing year sees changes— new rides are added, another layer of paint is applied, and the sea of memories swells.

The Boardwalk is forever entwined with the heart and soul of Santa Cruz. More than a thrilling amusement park ride or a vital part of the economy, the Boardwalk is the repository for the town's memories. It is the focal point of Santa Cruz's history and geography. And those who have been a part of this marvelous creation can look back and truly say, "Never a Dull Moment."

Plate 161 ~ 1980's in Santa Cruz. [Courtesy of the Harold J. van Gorder Collection]

Plate 162 ~ Ferriswheel. 1960. [Courtesy of the Harold J. van Gorder Collection]

Plate 163 ~ The new skyglider aerial ride traveled the length of the Boardwalk. 1967 Postcard. [Courtesy of the Harold J. van Gorder Collection]

Plate 164 ~ "Open Air Beach Theater." 60s Postcard. [Courtesy of the Harold J. van Gorder Collection]

Plate 165 ~ "Paul Penna at the Boardwalk." [Courtesy of Daisy Rose Gandolfi]

Endnotes

1. Olin, L.G. *The Development and Promotion of Santa Cruz Tourism*, MA thesis, San Jose State College, 1967, p.22.

2. Ibid.

3. "One Day in San Francisco," *Santa Cruz Daily Surf*, (November 12, 1903): p.1.

4. Payne, Stephen M. *Testimonies Collected About the Santa Cruz Boardwalk*, interview with Warren (Skip) Littlefield,(3/5/1971): P.25.

5. Ibid.

6. "At Neptune Grill," *Santa Cruz Daily Surf*, (June 13, 1904): p. 1.

7. van Gorder, Harold J. "Summer on the Beach," *Now and Then*, (June 29, 1989).

8. Payne, Stephen M. *Testimonies Collected About the Santa Cruz Boardwalk*, (April 26, 1972), interview with unidentified female, 85 years old, and ex-Boardwalk worker identified as #22.

9. *Santa Cruz Sentinel*, (June 23, 1906): p.1.

10. Payne, Stephen M. *Testimonies Collected About the Santa Cruz Boardwalk*, (April 26, 1972), interview with identified female, 85 years old, and ex-Boardwalk worker identified as #22.

11. Chase, John. *Sidewalk Companion to Santa Cruz Architecture*, Paper Vision Press,)1979): p.36.

12. Rothbuchen, Jessica. *Santa Cruz Boardwalk Business*, University of California Santa Cruz Humanities 61, (6/8/1984): p.3.

13. *Santa Cruz Beach Boardwalk Beach News*. Santa Cruz Seaside Company, Santa Cruz, California, (January 2002).

14. Rothbuchen, Jessica. *Santa Cruz Boardwalk Business*. University of California Santa Cruz Humanities 61, (6/8/1984): p.4.

15. "Casino Ballroom Nearing Completion." *Santa Cruz Yesterdays, Santa Cruz Sentinel*, (1907).

16. Payne, Stephen M. *Testimonies Collected About the Santa Cruz Boardwalk*, 1971, (April 26, 1972) interview with identified female, 85 years old, and ex-Boardwalk worker identified as #22.

17. van Gorder, Harold J. "Santa Cruz Plunge", from Now and Then, (July 27, 1989).

18. Anonymous. "On the Boardwalk: Decades of Thrills and Beauty." *San Jose Mercury, California Today Sunday Magazine*, (Oct 14, 1979): p. 16.

19. Payne, Stephen M. *Testimonies Collected About the Santa Cruz Boardwalk*, 1971, interview with Warren (Skip) Littlefield, (3/5/1971): p. 27

20. Littlefield, Warren (Skip). *The Plunge*. News and Notes from the Santa Cruz Historical Society, (June 1963), Number 25, Margaret Koch editor, p. 3

21. Rothbuchen, Jessica. *Santa Cruz Boardwalk Business*. University of California Santa Cruz Humanities 61, (6/8/1984), not published, p. 4, interview with Mrs. Howe.

22. Payne, Stephen M. *Testimonies Collected About the Santa Cruz Boardwalk*. Stephen M. Payne, 17390 Highway 9, Boulder Creek, CA (3/5/1971). Interview with Warren "Skip" Littlefield 3/5/1971.

23. Payne, Stephen M. *Testimonies Collected About the Santa Cruz Boardwalk*, April 20, 1972, interview with identified male 62 years old, ex-Boardwalk worker identified as 12.

24. Payne, Stephen M. *Testimonies Collected About the Santa Cruz Boardwalk*, April 26, 1972 interview with identified male 47 years old, son of publicity director [probably Littlefield] identified as #3.

25. Littlefield, Warren (Skip). *The Plunge*. News and Notes from the Santa Cruz Historical Society, (June 1963): Number 25, Margaret Koch editor, p.3.

26. "On the Boardwalk: Decades of Thrills and Beauty," *SJ Mercury California Today Sunday Magazine*, (Oct 14, 1979): p. 16.

27. Rothbuchen, Jessica. *Santa Cruz Boardwalk Business*, University of California Santa Cruz Humanities 61, (6/8/1984): p 6, interview with Mrs. Howe.

28. "Orand Gift Promenade," *Santa Cruz Daily Surf*, (June 21, 1909): p.2.

29. Ibid.

30. "Spectacular Casino Illumination," *Santa Cruz Yesterdays*, (May 29, 1949).

31. Rothbuchen, Jessica. *Santa Cruz Boardwalk Business*. University of California Santa Cruz Humanities 61, (6/8/1984): p.7.

32. "Original Face of the Beach Natatorium in 1909," *Santa Cruz Yesterdays*, no date.

33. "The Season Is Opened," *Santa Cruz Daily Surf*, (June 10, 1912): p.1.

34. "Great Treat for Santa Cruz," *Santa Cruz Daily Surf*, (March 15, 1912).

35. "What Shall Be," *Santa Cruz Daily Surf*, (August 7, 1906): p.2.

36. Payne, Stephen M. *Testimonies Collected About the Santa Cruz Boardwalk*, 1971, April 26, 1972 interview with identified female, 85 years old, and ex-Boardwalk worker identified as #22.

37. Ibid.

38. Chase, John. "Swanton's Folly," *The Santa Cruz Weekly*, (November 19, 1980).

39. Anonymous. "Proposed Week End Program of Entertainment," Santa Cruz Daily Surf, (December 12, 1908): p.1.

40. "Bathers Not To Lounge," *Santa Cruz Daily Surf*, (June 26, 1911): p. 4.

41. Tipton, Felicia S. *The Casa Del Rey Hotel: Looking at Its Past to Understand Its Present*, University of California Santa Cruz E.S. 143 Research Project, Design of the Built Environment, Professor Paul Neibank, (June 6, 1988): p.1.

42. "Casa Del Rey," *Santa Cruz Daily Surf*, (June 27, 1911): p.2.

43. "Queen Clara Walti and Her Court, 1912 Water Pageant," *Santa Cruz Yesterdays*. No date.

44. "Pageant — ship of lights, 1912," *Santa Cruz Yesterdays*, (January 27, 1957).

45. "Bathing Suits Sold for Rags," *Santa Cruz Daily Surf*, (June 11, 1913): p. 1.

46. "Bidding on Lease of Beach Company Plant," *Santa Cruz Sentinel*, (May 27, 1914): p.1.

47. "Confidence is Restored in Santa Cruz," *Santa Cruz Daily Surf*, (May 27, 1914): p. 1.

48. "Construction and Amusement Contracts," *Santa Cruz Daily Surf*, (January 28, 1914): p. 1.

49. Wills, Catherine Alexandra. *Allusions of Grandeur: Restoring the Santa Cruz Boardwalk*, Catherine Alexandra Wills, Simmons College, Masters Thesis, UC Berkeley, (1971): p.18

50. Olin, L.G. *The Development and Promotion of Santa Cruz Tourism*, MA thesis, San Jose State College, (1967): p.67

51. "Santa Cruz Seaside Company," *Santa Cruz Daily Surf*, (February 15, 1916): p.1.

52. Ibid.

53. "Out of it," *Santa Cruz Daily Surf*, (April 22, 1916): p.1.

54. van Gorder, Harold J. "Child Labor Moments," *Now and Then*, (October 12, 1989).

55. "Fourth at the Beach," *Santa Cruz Daily Surf*, (July 5, 1914): p.3.

56. Stone, George W. "Timely Topics," *Santa Cruz Sentinel*, (June 6, 1919): p.3.

57. "Record Breaker At the Plunge," *Santa Cruz Sentinel*, (July 5, 1919): p.3.

58. "Social," *Santa Cruz Sentinel*, (July 4, 1919): p. 4.

59. "Ball at Casino," *Santa Cruz Sentinel*, (July 10, 1919): p.5.

60. "Hotels, Lodging Houses Crowded to the Very Limit," *Santa Cruz Sentinel*, (July 5, 1919): p. 1.

61. "Over 20,000 Visitors in Santa Cruz," *Santa Cruz Evening News,* (July 5, 1919): p.4.

62. "Girls Happy at Chance to Reach Saloon's Inside," *Santa Cruz Evening News*, (July 10, 1919): p.4

63. "Propeller Parts in Air," *Santa Cruz Evening News*,(July 6, 1920): p. 5.

64. "Natatorium Opens for Season at Beach," *Santa Cruz Daily Surf,* (April 18, 1920).

65. "Chamber Rooms 3,000 Visitors," *Santa Cruz Evening News*, (July 6, 1920): p.5.

66. Hooper, Linda Rosewood. *Interview with Haswell Leask.*

67. "Too Much Makeup, Too Much Skin," *San Jose Mercury News*, (June 7, 1994): p.1B.

68. "Monday a Busy Day at Beach," *Santa Cruz Evening News*, (June 28, 1921): p.5.

69. Ibid.

70. "John Tait Outlines Beach Front Deal," *Santa Cruz Evening News*, (October 18, 1921): p.1.

71. "Thirty-one Unlocked Toilets at Beach, Says Royce; Beach Company Won't be Dictated to He Says; Mayor Talks," *Santa Cruz Evening News,* (July 17, 1923): p.4.

72. "Dodgem Ride Will Be Newest Beach Front Feature; Summer Plans," *Santa Cruz Evening News*, (January 23, 1923): p.5.

73. "Barn Dance, Deep Sea Wedding," *Santa Cruz Evening News*, (October 8, 1922): p. 5.

74. Ibid.

75. Ibid.

76. Advertisement, *Santa Cruz Evening News*, (June 25, 1923): p.6.

77. "Beach Attractions for my Summer Vacation," *Santa Cruz Evening News*, (July 13, 1923): p.7.

78. Anonymous. "Life on the Ocean Wave in Old-Time Bathing Suits, Thinking Back. Ralph Miller spins a few yarns," *Santa Cruz Morning News*, (July 14, 1923): p.6.

79. Ibid.

80. "Largest Giant Dipper on Pacific Coast Will Begin Operation Saturday," *Santa Cruz Evening News*, (May 15, 1924): p.7.

81. Ibid.

82. Ibid.

83. "Casino Coffee Shop Opening and Grand Ball Start Season," *Santa Cruz Evening News*, (May 16, 1924): p.3.

84. Ibid.

85. "Beach Opening is Occasion for Much Mirth and Gaiety," *Santa Cruz Evening News*, (May 19, 1924): p.10.

86. "Beach Opening is Occasion for Much Mirth and Gaiety," *Santa Cruz Evening News*, (May 19, 1924): p.10.

87. "Vacation Official Santa Cruz Beach Front Amusement Information," *Santa Cruz Evening News*, (August 5 and 12, 1924): p.10.

88. Vacation. Advertisement, *Santa Cruz Evening News*, (June 25): p. 12; (June 30): p. 10; (July 2, 1925): p. 10.

89. "Boardwalk discussed by Chamber of Commerce; Project Heartily endorsed," *Santa Cruz Morning News*, (January 12, 1926): p.3.

90. "Pappas Charges Discrimination as Council Holds Up Bath Permit and Hints Condemnation," *Santa Cruz Evening News*, (May 13, 1926): p.8.

91. Ibid.

92. Ibid.

93. Ibid.

94. "Announcements," *Santa Cruz Evening News*, (October 24, 1926): p. 7.

95. Vacation. Advertisement, *Santa Cruz Evening News*, (August 17, 1926): p. 9.

96. Samuel Leask Advertisement, *Santa Cruz Evening News*, (July 14, 1926): p.3.

97. "Carnival Dance at "Dreamland" This Evening," *Santa Cruz Evening News*, (January 1, 1927).

98. "Wind and Waves Strike Santa Cruz Shore," *Santa Cruz Evening News*, "February 12, 1926"): p.1.

99. "Coleman Buys Pappas Property," *Santa Cruz Evening News*, (March 10, 1927): p.1.

100. "Santa Cruz Is Drab, Backwards Rotary Hears," *Santa Cruz Evening News*, (March 18, 1927): p.1.

101. Ibid.

102. "Vote Landslide Sweeps Fred W. Swanton Into Mayor's Chair At First Election," *Santa Cruz Evening News*, (May 4, 1927): p.1.

103. "Trained Fleas on Board Walk," *Santa Cruz Evening News*, (May 25, 1927(): p.10.

104. "Lantern Carnival Program Now All Arranged," *Santa Cruz Evening News*, (June 6, 1927): p.2.

105. "Public Meeting Reveals Condition of Great Beach Front Industry; Santa Cruzans on Directorate," *Santa Cruz Evening News*, (February 25, 1928): p.3.

106. "Casa del Rey Opens Beautiful Spanish Gardens to Public," *Santa Cruz Evening News*, (March 30, 1928): p.5.

107. Ham Tree Restaurant. Advertisement. *Santa Cruz Evening News,* (June 8, 1928): p. 10.

108. "City Asked to Provide Police Officer," *Santa Cruz Evening News*, (July 18, 1928): p.3.

109. "Council and Beach Company," *Santa Cruz Evening News*, (July 13, 1928): p.1.

110. "Oakland Man Makes First Airplane Landing on Santa Cruz Beach," *Santa Cruz Evening News*, (December 24, 1928): p.3.

111. "Plans for New Beach Resort Are Approved," *Santa Cruz Evening News*, (May 31, 1930): p.8.

112. "Seaside Co. Prepares Beach Front Fight," *Santa Cruz Evening News*, (August 29, 1930): p.1.

113. "City Moves to Force Beach Company," *Santa Cruz Evening News*, (August 7, 1930): p.1.

114. "Mayor States Beach Report is a Mistake," *Santa Cruz Evening News*, (September 29, 1931): p.7.

115. "S.C. Seaside Co Directors All Are Re-elected," *Santa Cruz Evening News*, (February 27, 1932): p.5.

116. "Gala Opening of Casa Del Rey Friday," *Santa Cruz Evening News*, (June 26, 1932): p.10.

117. "Here's Preview of Monday's Beach Garb Display," *Santa Cruz Evening News*, (April 22, 1932): p.1; and "Coast-Wide Interest Roused by Bathing Suit Test Display on Santa Cruz Beach Monday," (April 23, 1932): p.1; and "City Dads Digesting Data From Bathing Suit Review Before Drafting New Beach Ordinance," *Santa Cruz Evening News*, (April 26, 1932): p.2.

118. "City to Press Beach Title Court Suit," *Santa Cruz Evening News*, (May 10, 1932): p.1.

119. "Swanton Pledges S.C. Cleanup," *Santa Cruz Evening News*, (May 23, 1932): p.1.

120. "Big Ship off Pier to Lure Visitors," *Santa Cruz Evening News*, (May 22, 1933): p.1.

121. "Micky Malto Celebration Set for Boardwalk," *Santa Cruz Evening News*, (July 19, 1933): p.5.

122. "Over $15,000 Being Spent By the Casa del Rey on Improvements," *Santa Cruz Evening News*, (November 10, 1933): p.6.

123. "Admission Day Week-End Fete Set for Beach," *Santa Cruz Evening News*, (September 4).

124. "Riptide," *Santa Cruz Evening News*, (March 5, 1935): p.3.

125. Ibid.

126. Ibid.

127. Ibid.

128. "Woman Tells of Accident in Testimony," *Santa Cruz Evening News*, (September 16, 1936): p.2.

129. "High Business Mark Hit in August for Casa del Rey Under Troyers," *Santa Cruz Evening News*, (September 18, 1935): p.1.

130. "Noted Colored Band Plays in S.C. Tonight," *Santa Cruz Evening News*, (November 28, 1936): p.6.

131. "Await Piles For Café On City Beach," *Santa Cruz Evening News*, (November 11, 1938): p.2.

132. "Seaside Company Embarks On Biggest Improvement Program Undertaken In Last 12 Years," *Santa Cruz Sentinel*, (January 21, 1940): p.1.

133. "Indian Fire Eater," *Santa Cruz Sentinel*, (August 30, 1941): p.5.

134. *Santa Cruz Evening News*, (December 21, 1941): p.1.

135. "Red Wallace Was A Swimming Great," *Santa Cruz Sentinel*, (March 26, 1943): p.4.

136. Ibid.

137. Ibid.

138. Clark, Karen, "Santa Cruz Boardwalk a Survivor, Boardwalk Blends Old With New, Boardwalk has Tons of Memorabilia," *Santa Cruz Sentinel*, (January 29, 1991).

Research Materials

Boardwalk Timeline

1864	Long Branch Baths opened by Mary Liddell and son Alfred
1865	Other bathhouses operating at this time nearby, most names lost
1868	John and David Leibbrandt open Dolphin Baths at mouth of San Lorenzo River; Leibbrandts build first boardwalk along waterfront to access their baths
1870s	Henry Cowell begins series of lawsuits to buy private right to waterfront, Californians travel to Santa Cruz via steamboats; Douglas House built (later Sea Beach)
1872	Legislation passed to keep waterfront open to the public
1875	John Leibbrandt collapses during marathon swim, becomes bedridden, eventually leads to his death
1879	A.F. Wheaton builds baths where Casino now stands
1885	Capt. Charles Frederick Miller buys out Wheaton and opens Neptune Baths
1886	Reference to the roller-coaster in the newspaper; Sea Beach Hotel completed (formerly Douglas House)
1887	Capt. James Miller (son of Charles) opens Neptune House, a restaurant and shell shop next door to Neptune Baths
1889	Miller and Leibbrandts join forces to create Dolphin-Neptune hybrid; Capt. Fred Miller goes to sea, leaves baths in hands of brothers
1903	Theodore Roosevelt visits; Santa Cruz Beach, Cottage and Tent City Corporation formed

1904	Plunge Bath opens under Swanton; New Neptune Casino opened by Fred Swanton; Neptune and Dolphin razed
1906	Neptune Casino burns; Santa Cruz Beach, Cottage, and Tent City becomes Santa Cruz Beach Company; Republican Convention held in Santa Cruz
1908	Thompson's Scenic Railway (original coaster)
1909	Neptune Casino reopened with Aquarium, Cocoanut Grove Ballroom, new Natatorium, new Pleasure Pier, skating rink turned into dance pavilion
1910	Looff Carousel, Casa del Rey Hotel built
1912	Sea Beach Hotel burns, Beach Company goes bankrupt, closes for three years
1916	Seaside Company purchases all assets of the SCBCTC; Reopens under Waldo Coleman, Swanton disposes of his stock
1917	Hwy. 17 resurfaced, auto traffic to Santa Cruz increases
1918	Charles Looff dies in New York, first parking lot for Boardwalk
1924	Thompson's railway demolished; Giant Dipper built, also first three fatalities. First Miss California pageant held at Boardwalk
1926	Seaside buys Southern Pacific's interest in Casa del Rey
1927	Fred Swanton elected Mayor
1930s	Suntan Special Railroad, Big Band era, decline in number of amusement parks
1934	Ballroom named Cocoanut Grove
1940	Slide for Life ride closed by Industrial Accident Commission, fatality on Dipper, Fred Swanton dies
1943	Jenkins, Williamson and Howe running Seaside Co.
1940s	Boardwalk leased to US Navy for water safety instruction, Casa del Rey used as hospital
1945	Last Plunge Water Carnival held on Labor Day
1946	Casa del Rey returned to public, bought by private company
1950s	Television, Disneyland opens, carousel ring arm mechanized, Seaside Co. begins to repair and reinvest
1952	Laurence Canfield becomes President of Seaside Company
1955	Wild Mouse built

1956	Last Suntan Special
1958	Canvas carousel clown retired, then brought back due to popular demand, Wild Mouse built
1960	Original carousel house demolished, new house built, Casa del Rey becomes retirement home
1961	Expansion of eastern end of park, 3.5 acres, Cave Train added
1962	Natatorium closed, miniature golf course built over it/in its place, Pleasure Pier dismantled
1965	Last Miss California held at Boardwalk
1972	Dipper fatality, height requirements instated, metal bumper cars replaced w/ fiberglass
1976	Dipper repainted
1977	Wild Mouse closed, replaced by Jet Star
1979	Fireworks tradition ended
1980s	Carousel horses renovated
1984	Charles Canfield II becomes Seaside Company President, Seaside Co. buys Casa del Rey
1987	Giant Dipper and Looff Carousel made National Historical Landmarks
1988	Outdoor concerts launched in the shell stage
1989	Loma Prieta Earthquake, Casa del Rey damaged beyond repair, area becomes parking lot.
1991	Jet Star torn down, replaced by Hurricane, carousel organ restored, Neptune's Kingdom opened (video arcade)
1996	Suntan Special revived (train)
2000	Cave Train redesigned

Boardwalk Presidents

1903-1907 Henry Willey (Santa Cruz Beach, Cottage, and Tent City Corporation)

1907-1915 John Martin (Santa Cruz Company)

1916-1928 S. Waldo Coleman (Santa Cruz Seaside Company & Beach Hotel Company)

1928-1933 Robert L. Cardiff

1933-1943 James R. Williamson

1943-1951 Louis Jenkins

1952-1984 Laurence Canfield

1984-Present Charles Canfield II

Referenced Materials

- Beal, Chandra. *Splash Acorss Texas! The Definitive Guide to Swimming in Central Texas*, La Luna Publishing, Austin, Texas, 1999.

- Beal, Richard. *Highway 17 – The Road to Santa Cruz*, The Pacific Group, Aptos, California, 1991.

- Burton, Robert and Thomas McHugh. Samuel Leask: Transplanted Scot Citizen Par Excellence. 1964.

- Chase, John. *Sidewalk Companion to Santa Cruz Architecture*, Paper Vision Press, 1979.

- Chase, John. <u>Swanton's Folly</u>, *The Santa Cruz Weekly*, Nov 19, 1980.

- Clark, Donald Thomas. *Santa Cruz County Place Names*, Santa Cruz Historical Society, 1986.

- Gibson, Ross Eric. *Empire of the Casa del Rey: An historic perspective report on the Casa del Rey & La Bahia*, 1997.

- Hooper, Linda Rosewood. Interview with Haswell Leask, no date.

- Judah, H.R., Jr. *At Santa Cruz by the Sea*, June 1907, v. 19:2 p. 171.

- Koch, Margaret. *Santa Cruz County, Parade of the Past*, Valley Publishers, Fresno, CA, 1973.

- Lam, Charlie. *Charles Looff, Arthur Looff, and the Giant Dipper*, University of California Santa Cruz, Humanities 61, Charles Atkinson, unpublished and undated.

- Littlefield, Skip. Beach Music – Casino Ballroom/Cocoanut Grove, Santa Cruz Seaside Company, interoffice memorandum, August 31, 1977.

- Littlefield, Skip. *Santa Cruz Wharves*, 1962.

- Littlefield, Skip. *The Plunge, News and Notes from the Santa Cruz Historical Society*, June 1963, Number 25,

- Littlefield, Skip. Vintage Arcade Machines, Santa Cruz Beach Boardwalk interoffice communication, July 3, 1981.

- Mathilda, Aunt. *Footsteps on the Sands of Time: The County's Pioneer Legion*, Riptide Biographical Notes, Santa Cruziana oversize, Nov 2, 1950,

- McHugh Scrapbook, Number 1. Xerox of a scrapbook of newspaper articles.

- Olin, L.G. The Development and Promotion of Santa Cruz Tourism, MA thesis, San Jose State College, 1967

- Payne, Stephen M. It's Better Than Slopping Hamburgers: Oral Traditions of the Santa Cruz Boardwalk, University of California Santa Cruz Anthropology 195, Senior Thesis, Dr. Gary Gossen, Anthropology Board of Studies. GV/54/C22/S3633/1972a.

- Payne, Stephen M. Testimonies Collected About the Santa Cruz Boardwalk, March 5, 1971.

- Perry, Frank. Lighthouse Point: Illuminating Santa Cruz, Otter B Books, Santa Cruz, California, 2002.

- Rothbuchen, Jessica. Santa Cruz Boardwalk Business, University of California Santa Cruz Humanities 61, June 8, 1984

- Rowland, Leon. Scrapbook Vol. 2, from his local history column "The Circuit Rider" published 1930-1950 in the Santa Cruz News and later the Santa Cruz Sentinel.

- Sawyer, Preston. Preston Sawyer Collection of photos. UCSC Special Collections Library.

- Schiffrin, Andrew. Santa Cruz Boardwalk: Survival of the Funnest. California Waterfront Age, spring 1986, Vol. 2, No. 2.

- Tipton, Felicia S. The Casa Del Rey Hotel: Looking at Its Past to Understand Its Present, University of California Santa Cruz E.S. 143 Research Project, Design of the Built Environment, Professor Paul Niebanck, June 6, 1988.

- van Gorder, Harold J. Child Labor Memories, Now and Then, October 12, 1989.

- van Gorder, Harold J. Personal interviews with the author, summer 2002.

- van Gorder, Harold J. Santa Cruz Plunge, Now and Then, July 27, 1989.

- van Gorder, Harold J. School's Out for the Summer, Now and Then, July 13, 1989.

- van Gorder, Harold J. Summer on the Beach, Now and Then, June 29, 1989.
- van Gorder, Harold J. Letter to Richard Beal, April 11, 2003.
- Vescia, Paolo. Beachflats: black and white gelatin silver prints, Santa Cruz, CA, 1986.
- Wills, Catherine Alexandra. Allusions of Grandeur: Restoring the Santa Cruz Boardwalk, Simmons College, Masters Thesis, UC Berkeley, Oversize Santa Cruziana, 1971.

Newspaper Articles

- "$20,000 Scenic Railway," *Santa Cruz Daily Surf*, (April 7, 1908): p. 6.

- "$50,000 Suit Against Beach Company Settled," *Santa Cruz Evening News*, (September 3, 1937): p3.

- "$6,000 To Be Spent on Cocoanut Grove," *Santa Cruz Evening News*, (March 3, 1937): p.1.

- "1,000 Kids Scramble For Easter Eggs," *Santa Cruz Sentinel*, (April 14, 1942): p.2.

- "16,000 is Peak Crowd At Beach Over Weekend," *Santa Cruz Evening News*, (July 29, 1930): p.10.

- "2 hours 20 minutes from San Francisco," *Santa Cruz Daily Surf*, (June 7, 1912): p. 1.

- "2,721 Bath Tickets," *Santa Cruz Daily Surf*, (July 5, 1917): p. 3.

- "2:18 A.M. "Alert" Locally," *Santa Cruz Evening News*, (December 10, 1944): p1.

- "20,000 Here for Week-End Shows Business Increases," *Santa Cruz Evening News*, (May 7, 1934): p.1.

- "5000 Cars Bound to Santa Cruz Pass Through Los Gatos," *Santa Cruz Evening News*, (August 29, 1921): p. 4.

- "75th Anniversary of the Boardwalk," *San Jose Mercury* (5/18/99).

- "A Brilliant Banquet and Ball," *Santa Cruz Daily Surf* (June 19, 1916).

- "A Change in Speed," *Santa Cruz Daily Surf*, (June 22, 1904): p. 1.

- "A Contract to Outfit New Chutes at Beach," *Santa Cruz Evening News*, (May 18, 1929): p.11.

- "A Pier for Pleasure," *Santa Cruz Daily Surf*, (January 26, 1904): p. 1.

- "A Profile of the Proposed Beach Improvements and Cottage and Tent City," *Santa Cruz Daily Surf*, (October 18, 1903): p. 1.

- "A Royal Record Maker" *Santa Cruz Daily Surf*, (June 5, 1911): p.1.

- "Admission Day Program at Beach," *Santa Cruz Evening News*, (September 8, 1934): p.1.

- "Admission Day Week-End Fete Set for Beach," *Santa Cruz Evening News*, (September 4).

- "Air Ships Ready for Passenger Travel," *Santa Cruz Evening News*, (July 3, 1920): p. 1.

- "Announcement," *Santa Cruz Evening News*, (October 24, 1926): p.7.

- "Annual Easter Egg Hunt," *Santa Cruz Evening News*, (April 16, 1935): p.1.

- "Aquarium Opening," *Santa Cruz Daily Surf,* (March 16, 1908): p. 3.

- "Aquarium Site Deal Confirmed," *Santa Cruz Evening News*, (May 1, 1939): p.1.

- "Aquatic Stars of S.F. For Race Here," *Santa Cruz Evening News*, (September 7, 1934): p.2.

- "Arthur Looff Points the Way: Invests Heavily in C of C," *Santa Cruz Evening News*, (May 10, 1924): p.1.

- "At Neptune Grill," *Santa Cruz Daily Surf,* (June 13, 1904): p. 1.

- "At the Beach," *Santa Cruz Daily Surf,* (Feb 7, 1905): p. 1.

- "At the Beach," *Santa Cruz Daily Surf,* (June 19, 1904): p. 1.

- "Auto Parking at the Beach," *Santa Cruz Daily Surf,* (July 8, 1918): p. 3.

- "Await Piles For Café On City Beach," *Santa Cruz Evening News*, (November 11, 1938): p.2.

- "Ball at Casino," *Santa Cruz Sentinel,* (July 10, 1919): p.5.

- "Balloon Race Set for Surf," *Santa Cruz Evening News*, (August 29, 1936): p.2.

- "Banner Beach Season is Shown by Seaside Firm," *Santa Cruz Evening News*, (February 26, 1937): p.1.

- "Barn Dance, Deep Sea Wedding," *Santa Cruz Evening News*, (October 8, 1922): p. 5.

- "Bathers Not To Lounge," *Santa Cruz Daily Surf,* (June 26, 1911): p. 4.

- "Bathing Suits Sold for Rags," *Santa Cruz Daily Surf,* (June 11, 1913): p. 1.

- "Bay Swell Cancels Naval Smoker; Strands Sailors," *Santa Cruz Evening News*, (November 11, 1937): p.1.

- "Beach Apartments of Casa del Rey To Have Rate Cut," *Santa Cruz Evening News*, (September 6, 1934): p.6.

- "Beach Attractions for my Summer Vacation," *Santa Cruz Evening News*, (July 13, 1923): p.7.

- "Beach Attractions for my Summer Vacation," *Santa Cruz Evening News*, (August 3, 1923): p.8.

- "Beach Band to Make Initial Bow Tomorrow," *Santa Cruz Evening News*, (April 1, 1933): p.2.

- "Beach Boardwalk Boasts 3 New Rides for 1940 Season,)" *Santa Cruz Sentinel*, (April 4, 1940): p.2.

- "Beach Branch Library" *Santa Cruz Daily Surf*, (August 3, 1918): p. 3.

- "Beach Building Plan Ready if Tenants Found," *Santa Cruz Evening News*, (June 20, 1933): p.2.

- "Beach Co. Will Defend," *Santa Cruz Evening News*, (June 24, 1930): p.1.

- "Beach Co. To Pay Its Water Bill to City" *Santa Cruz Sentinel*, (May 28, 1914): p.1.

- "Beach Concession Sold to Minnesotan by Nate Aboudara," *Santa Cruz Evening News*, (February 27, 1937): p.2.

- "Beach Front Ownership," *Santa Cruz Daily Surf*, (January 7, 1911): p. 1.

- "Beach Improvements on a Big Scale," *Santa Cruz Daily Surf*, (September 15, 1906): p. 1.

- "Beach Improvements" *Santa Cruz Daily Surf*, (August 30, 1904): p. 1.

- "Beach Mimic Scores," *Santa Cruz Evening News*, (August 7, 1937): p.2.

- "Beach Opening is Occasion for Much Mirth and Gaiety," *Santa Cruz Evening News*, (May 19, 1924): p.10.

- "Beach Parking Problem Again Before Council," *Santa Cruz Evening News*, (March 13, 1923): p.4.

- "Beach Quarantine Does Not Affect Plunge Location," *Santa Cruz Evening News*, (March 14, 1925): p.4.

- "Beautiful Santa Cruz County: a faithful reproduction in print and photography of its climate, capabilities, and beauties," *H.S. Crocker Company*, San Francisco, (1896).

- "Beer Garden At Beach Opened by "Hot Dog" Miller," *Santa Cruz Evening News*, (July 1, 1933): p.2.

- "Bidding on Lease of Beach Company Plant," *Santa Cruz Sentinel*, (May 27, 1914): p.1.

- "Big S.P. Band to be at Beach for Week-End," *Santa Cruz Evening News*, (June 14, 1933): p.2.

- "Big Ship off Pier to Lure Visitors," *Santa Cruz Evening News*, (May 22, 1933): p.1.

- "Boardwalk discussed by Chamber of Commerce; Project Heartily endorsed," *Santa Cruz Morning News*, (January 12, 1926): p.3.

- "Boardwalk Is Repaired," *Santa Cruz Sentinel*, (April 27, 1941): p.1.

- "Boardwalk plans birthday bash: 90 years of fun," *Santa Cruz Sentinel*, (May 22, 1997): p. A1.

- "Boardwalk to Get New Surface for Crowds of 1934," *Santa Cruz Evening News*, (February 12, 1934): p.3.

- "Boy Stands Up In Giant Dipper and Is Hurt in Fall," *Santa Cruz Evening News*, (September 24, 1934): p.2.

- "Bratwurstgroecklein," *Santa Cruz Daily Surf*, (March 11, 1908).

- "Breakers Roar "Well Done" as Miller Fetes Beach Milestone," *Santa Cruz Evening News*, (April 20, 1938): p.2.

- "Building Trades Declaration Against Seaside Company Repudiated by Carpenters," *Santa Cruz Morning News*, (June 14, 1921): p. 1.

- "Burning of Ship Will be Repeated At Beach Tonight," *Santa Cruz Evening News*, (July 8, 1933) p.2.

- "California's Gold #205, "Santa Cruz," Huell Howser Productions, 1991," *Santa Cruz Library video tape*, (11/16/2001).

- "Cardiff Again Elected Head of Seaside Co," *Santa Cruz Evening News*, (February 28, 1931) p.7.

- "Cardiff Renamed President of S.C. Seaside Company," *Santa Cruz Evening News*, (March 1, 1930): p.1.

- "Carnival Dance at "Dreamland" This Evening," *Santa Cruz Evening News*, (January 1, 1927).

- "Carnival Night at Casino Ballroom Next Saturday," *Santa Cruz Evening News*, (April 14, 1933): p.2.

- "Carona Drowning Said Accidental," *Santa Cruz Evening News*, (April 21, 1937): p.3.

- "Casa del Rey (The House of the King) Santa Cruz, California," *UC Special Collections*

- "Casa del Rey Decision Comes at Today's Meeting," *Santa Cruz Evening News*, (April 25, 1923).

- "Casa Del Rey Gardens Present Pretty Appearance," *Santa Cruz Evening News*, (May 6, 1921): p. 2.

- "Casa del Rey Hotel Leased for Summer," *Santa Cruz Evening News*, (February 2, 1932): p.3.

- "Casa del Rey Lease Renewed by Troyers," *Santa Cruz Evening News*, (April 4, 1933): p.3.

- "Casa del Rey Lease Sought by Rohlfs," *Santa Cruz Evening News*, (February 12, 1931): p.1.

- "Casa del Rey Opening Plans Nearly Ready," *Santa Cruz Evening News*, (June 20, 1932): p.2.

- "Casa del Rey Opens Beautiful Spanish Gardens to Public," *Santa Cruz Evening News*, (March 30, 1928): p.5.

- "Casa del Rey Season Plans Are Announced," *Santa Cruz Evening News*, (May 11, 1932): p.1.

- "Casa del Rey to Remain Open," *Santa Cruz Evening News*, (September 4, 1926): p.8.

- "Casa Del Rey. Advertisement," *Santa Cruz Sentinel*, (April 23, 1920): p. 6.

- "Casa Del Rey," *Santa Cruz Daily Surf*, (June 27, 1911): p. 2.

- "Casa del Rey: Casino and Beach, Santa Cruz, California," *Color pamphlet*, no date or publisher.

- "Casino Coffee Shop Opening and Grand Ball Start Season," *Santa Cruz Evening News*, (May 16, 1924): p.3.

- "Casino Improvements," *Santa Cruz Daily Surf*, (May 23, 1917): p. 4.

- "Casino Opening," *Santa Cruz Daily Surf*, (June 30, 1917): p. 4.

- "Casino Opening," *Santa Cruz Daily Surf*, (June 8, 1912): p. 4.

- "Casino Restaurant Will Open Season; New Management," *Santa Cruz Evening News*, (May 14, 1927): p.7.

- "Casino to Hold 20 Years After Fete June 10-12," *Santa Cruz Evening News*, (June 1, 1927): p. 2.

- "Chamber Rooms 3,000 Visitors," *Santa Cruz Evening News*, (July 6, 1920): p. 5.

- "Charles Canfield Has a Scheme to Raise More Revenue," *Santa Cruz Evening News*, (July 18, 1921): p. 3.

- "Chute the Chutes to be erected at Beach," *Santa Cruz Evening News*, (March 27, 1929): p.8.

- "City Asked to Provide Police Officer," *Santa Cruz Evening News*, (July 18, 1928): p.3.

- "City Attorney Gives Opinion on Title of Casino to Site," *Santa Cruz Evening News*, (July 14, 1923): p.4.

- "City Attorney Reveals City Plans At Beach," *Santa Cruz Evening News*, (June 25, 1930): p.1.

- "City Beach Title to be Settled," *Santa Cruz Evening News*, (April 8, 1930): p.1.

- "City Council," *Santa Cruz Daily Surf*, (June 6, 1916): p. 8.

- "City Dads Digesting Data From Bathing Suit Review Before Drafting New Beach Ordinance," *Santa Cruz Evening News*, (April 26, 1932): p.2.

- "City Moves to Force Beach Company," *Santa Cruz Evening News*, (August 7, 1930): p.1.

- "City Sues for Beach Title, Not To Perfect Old Title, says Seaside Co. Attorney," *Santa Cruz Evening News*, (August 8, 1930): p.1.

- "City to Press Beach Title Court Suit," *Santa Cruz Evening News*, (May 10, 1932): p.1.

- "Clean up! Open up!" *Santa Cruz Daily Surf*, (June 2, 1916): p. 8.

- "Closing of the Casa del Rey," *Santa Cruz Evening News*, (September 19, 1930): p.12.

- "Coast-Wide Interest Roused by Bathing Suit Test Display on Santa Cruz Beach Monday," (April 23, 1932): p.1.

- "Coleman Again Seaside Co Director," *Santa Cruz Evening News*, (May 3, 1933): p.2.

- "Coleman Buys Pappas Property," *Santa Cruz Evening News*, (March 10, 1927): p.1.

- "Coleman in Command," *Santa Cruz Daily Surf*, (February 25, 1916): p. 1.

- "Coleman in Command," *Santa Cruz Daily Surf*, (February 26, 1916): p. 1.

- "Coleman Ready to Start Beach Front Improvement; Makes Offer to City," *Santa Cruz Evening News*, (February 26, 1926): p.1.

- "Coleman Retires from Presidency," *Santa Cruz Evening News*, (June 22, 1928): p.1.

- "Colorado Feted Here," *Santa Cruz Evening News*, (November 9, 1937): p.1.

- "Compromise Allows Pappas Bath Pavilion," *Santa Cruz Evening News*, (February 18, 1927): p.1.

- "Confidence is Restored in Santa Cruz," *Santa Cruz Daily Surf*, (May 27, 1914): p. 1.

- "Construction and Amusement Contracts," *Santa Cruz Daily Surf*, (January 28, 1914): p. 1.

- "Construction of New Casino," *Santa Cruz Daily Surf*, (October 22, 1906): p. 1.

- "Convention Hall," *Santa Cruz Daily Surf*, (August 13, 1906): p. 3.

- "Council and Beach Company," *Santa Cruz Evening News*, (July 13, 1928): p.1.

- "Covered Arch from Casa del Rey to Casino to be made by Bower of Blooms by Troyers," *Santa Cruz Evening News*, (March 9, 1932): p.2.

- "Dance Advertisement," *Santa Cruz Sentinel*, (June 6, 1919): p. 2.

- "Dedication Due for Flag Pole On Boardwalk," *Santa Cruz Sentinel*, (August 25, 1940): p.1.

- "Demurrer Filed in Plunge Fall," *Santa Cruz Evening News*, (November 10, 1936): p.2.

- "Diaz Features Water Carnival Saturday," *Santa Cruz Sentinel*, (August 21, 1943): p.4.

- "Dimout Restrictions Along Whole Pacific Coast Are Modified," *Santa Cruz Sentinel*, (October 10, 1943): p.1.

- "Dodgem Ride Will Be Newest Beach Front Feature; Summer Plans," *Santa Cruz Evening News*, (January 23, 1923): p.5.

- "Doings at the Beach," *Santa Cruz Daily Surf*, (January 7, 1904): p. 1.

- "Dormer, Belle, Scenes of Santa Cruz," Santa Cruz, CA, brochure, (1933).

- "Eight Hundred Coming With Democrats," *Santa Cruz Evening News*, (March 22, 1926): p.2.

- "Estimates Place 1,000,000 as Number of Persons in Santa Cruz During Past Summer," *Santa Cruz Evening News*, (September 6, 1930): p.9.

- "Exceeding Forty Thousand Dollars," *Santa Cruz Daily Surf*, (October 21, 1903): p. 1.

- "Extent of City's Ownership at Beach Once More Forms the Subject of Discussion," *Santa Cruz Evening News*, (May 14, 1931): p.5.

- "Fabulous Santa Cruz Plunge Water Carnival Splashes Into 44th Season," *Santa Cruz Sentinel*, (May 29, 1942): p.5.

- "Famous Benny Band Plays Here Tonight," *Santa Cruz Evening News*, (January 22, 1937): p.3.

- "Famous Dance Orchestra is to Play Here," *Santa Cruz Evening News*, (November 27, 1934): p.3.

- "Famous Divers, Amateurs, and Band To Be At Beach," *Santa Cruz Evening News*, (August 8, 1936): p.2.

- "Fire Destroys Concession," *Santa Cruz Evening News*, (March 9, 1927): p.2.

- "First Casino, Built Twenty Years Ago, Was Product of Sacrifice on Part of Men Who Conceived Idea," *Santa Cruz Morning News*, (June 13, 1924): p. 5.

- "First Suntan Due On May 18," *Santa Cruz Sentinel*, (April 23, 1941): p.1.

- "Five Bands to Play Here at Standard Fete," *Santa Cruz Evening News*, (September 15, 1937): p.3.

- "Fliers Soon to Drop on New Santa Cruz Field from Sky; Swanton Beach Site Selected," *Santa Cruz Evening News*, (July 1, 1924): p.1.

- "Flying Boat on Way to Santa Cruz," *Santa Cruz Evening News*, (July 2, 1920): p.1.

- "For the Summer," *Santa Cruz Daily Surf*, (May 10, 1905): p. 1.

- "Forgotten Strip of Beach Given to City by Harriet Blackburn," *Santa Cruz Evening News*, (June 18, 1935): p.1.

- "Forum Tonight on Boardwalk at the Chamber," *Santa Cruz Evening News*, (January 11, 1926): p.4.

- "Fourth at the Beach," *Santa Cruz Daily Surf*, (July 5, 1914): p.3.

- "Fred W. Swanton Dies," *Santa Cruz Evening News*, (September 4, 1940): p.1.

- "Gala Opening of Casa Del Rey Friday," *Santa Cruz Evening News*, (June 26, 1932): p.10.

- "Giant Dipper evolution had its ups, downs," *San Jose Mercury News*, (March 12, 1996): p. B1.

- "Giant Dipper May Be Property of Seaside Company," *Santa Cruz Evening News*, (June 13, 1933): p.3.

- "Girls Happy at Chance to Reach Saloon's Inside," *Santa Cruz Evening News*, (July 10, 1919): p.4.

- "Good Old Summer Time," *Santa Cruz Daily Surf*, (June 19, 1908): p.1.

- "Good Road Open Over Mountains," *Santa Cruz Evening News*, (May 21, 1920): p.1.

- "Good-bye, Old Paint," *Santa Cruz Sentinel*, (October 27, 1985): p.B1

- "Grand Plunge Carnival Ready for New Season," *Santa Cruz Sentinel*, (May 29, 1941): p.4.

- "Grandeur built along Boardwalk," *San Jose Mercury News*, (July 12, 1995): p. 1B.

- "Great Swimmers Draw an Immense Crowd," *Santa Cruz Sentinel*, (July 27, 1913).

- "Great Treat for Santa Cruz," *Santa Cruz Daily Surf*, (March 15, 1912).

- "Hall Leaving to Take Del Monte Berth," *Santa Cruz Evening News*, (June 18, 1927): p.1.

- "Hall Owes Seegars –Suntan On Watsonville Route Ups Traffic," *Santa Cruz Sentinel*, (August 1, 1940): p.1.

- "Halloween Dinner Dance Advertisement," *Santa Cruz Evening News*, (October 25, 10923): p.6.

- "Ham Tree Restaurant Advertisement," *Santa Cruz Evening News*, (June 8, 1928): p.10.

- "Here's Preview of Monday's Beach Garb Display," *Santa Cruz Evening News*, (April 22, 1932): p.1.

- "High Business Mark Hit in August for Casa del Rey Under Troyers," *Santa Cruz Evening News*, (September 18, 1935): p.1.

- "Holiday Crowd Breaks All Records for City," *Santa Cruz Sentinel*, (July 6, 1941): p.1.

- "Hollywood Came to Santa Cruz," *San Jose Mercury News*, (February 1, 1994): p. 1B.

- "Hot Pipe Burn Basis of Suit Against Hotel," *Santa Cruz Evening News*, (June 3, 1935): p.3.

- "Hotels, Lodging Houses Crowded to the Very Limit," *Santa Cruz Sentinel*, (July 5, 1919): p. 1.

- "Huge Beach Frolic Added to City Fete Plans," *Santa Cruz Evening News*, (September 18, 1935): p.1.

- "Huge Sunday Crowd Augurs," *Santa Cruz Evening News*, (July 2, 1934): p.1.

- "Hundreds Visit Fleet in Bay; Jackies Will See Trees; Coming Events," *Santa Cruz Evening News*, (June 28, 1921): p. 1.

- "Ideal Fish Restaurant In Expansion," *Santa Cruz Evening News*, (October 15, 1929): p.2.

- "Improvements at the Beach Have Begun," *Santa Cruz Evening News*, (February 9, 1939): p.1.

- "Indian Fire Eater," *Santa Cruz Sentinel*, (August 30, 1941): p.5.

- "Information Bureau at the Casino," *Santa Cruz Daily Surf*, (June 30, 1913): p.8.

- "J. Ross Whiting Promoted by Seaside Co," *Santa Cruz Evening News*, (January 7, 1935) p.2.

- "Joe Stagnaro to Sing At Bandstand," *Santa Cruz Sentinel*, (July 9, 1941): p.8.

- "John Tait Outlines Beach Front Deal," *Santa Cruz Evening News*, (October 18, 1921): p.1.

- "Judge Knight Takes Beach Title Suit Under Advisement," *Santa Cruz Evening News*, (October 18, 1921): p.1.

- "Kolb and Dill, Veteran Comedy Team," *Santa Cruz Evening News*, (December 4, 1934): p.1.

- "Lantern Carnival Program Now All Arranged," *Santa Cruz Evening News*, (June 6, 1927): p.2.

- "Large Crowds Coming to Casino Dance," *Santa Cruz Evening News*, (July 14, 1923): p.3.

- "Largest Giant Dipper on Pacific Coast Will Begin Operation Saturday," *Santa Cruz Evening News*, (May 15, 1924): p.7.

- "Latest Crowd of Season Here," *Santa Cruz Evening News*, (September 3, 1934): p.1.

- "Leading S.C. Developer Succumbs At Home Here," *Santa Cruz Evening News*, (September 3, 1940): p.1.

- "Life on the Ocean Wave in old-

- time bathing suits; thinking back Ralph Miller spins few yarns," *Santa Cruz Morning News*, (July 14, 1923): p.6.

- "List of Top 10 coasters," *New York Times*, (June 9, 1974).

- "Little boy badly hurt in beach mishap," *Santa Cruz Evening News*, (August 6, 1923): p.5.

- "Local Men Lease Garage at Beach," *Santa Cruz Evening News*, (February 7, 1925): p.8.

- "Local Representatives to Big Conference Learn How Santa Cruz and Northern California Is Selling," *Santa Cruz Evening News*, (February 19, 1923): p.2.

- "Long Miniature Railway Planned," *Santa Cruz Evening News*, (February 16, 1928): p.1.

- "Loop-o-plane New Thrill at Boardwalk," *Santa Cruz Evening News*, (April 3, 1937): p.3.

- "MacDonald Out as Manager at Casa del Rey," *Santa Cruz Evening News*, (May 22, 1928): p.3.

- "MacMurray in City," *Santa Cruz Evening News*, (September 16, 1936): p.1.

- "Malio Stagnaro to Put Big New Engine in Speedboat," *Santa Cruz Evening News*, (March 1, 1933) p.1.

- "Man Says He and Horse Took Spill From Merry-Go-Round," *Santa Cruz Sentinel*, (October 15, 1941): p.1.

- "Matthews to Succeed Hall in Events Job," *Santa Cruz Evening News*, (June 15, 1927): p.2.

- "May Pole Dance To Be Held at the Casino," *Santa Cruz Evening News*, (April 30, 1926): p.9.

- c

- "McNair Will Try for World Record At Plunge Tonight," *Santa Cruz Sentinel*, (August 9, 1941): p.5.

- "Micky Malto Celebration Set for Boardwalk," *Santa Cruz Evening News*, (July 19, 1933): p.5.

- "Miniature Railroad Completed," *Santa Cruz Evening News*, (March 31, 1928): p.1.

- "Monday a Busy Day at Beach," *Santa Cruz Evening News*, (June 28, 1921): p.5.

- "Monster Ground Swell Does Great Damage at Santa Cruz Beach Front," *Santa Cruz Evening News*, (September 21, 1938): p.3.

- "Moorish Casino Lured Boardwalk's Tourist Hordes," *Capitola Green Sheet*, (December 2, 1978): p.1.

- "More Details on Beach Deal," *Santa Cruz Evening News*, (October 19, 1921): p.1.

- "More lights for Beach Street," *Santa Cruz Evening News*, (June 21, 1928): p.2.

- "More Music at Beach," *Santa Cruz Evening News*, (July 29, 1920): p.1.

- "More Plans for Handling of Crowd," *Santa Cruz Evening News* (August 9, 1919): p.4.

- "Movies at the Beach," *Santa Cruz Daily Surf*, (July 21, 1914): p.8.

- "Name New Hostess for Casa del Rey," *Santa Cruz Evening News*, (January 17, 1929): p.10.

- "Natatorium Opens for Season at Beach," *Santa Cruz Daily Surf*, (April 18, 1920).

- "Nearby Cities Send Crowds to Santa Cruz as Result of Week End Boost Trip," *Santa Cruz Morning News*, (June 14, 1921): p.2.

- "New Beach Policy Results in Marked Improvements Everywhere," *Santa Cruz Evening News*, advertisement, (June 7, 1927): p.10; (June 14, 1927): p.9; (July 28, 1927): p.10.

- "New Idea Dance Pavilion," *Santa Cruz Daily Surf*, (April 28, 1908): p. 6.

- "New Record Crowd At Water Carnival As Stars Perform," *Santa Cruz Sentinel*, (July 13, 1941): p.5.

- "New Secretary-Treasurer of Seaside Co. is Named," *Santa Cruz Evening News*, (November 17, 1934): p.1.

- "New Submarine Anchors Here," *Santa Cruz Evening News*, (November 23, 1937)p.3.

- "News-Jantzen Swim Week To Have Record Crowds," *Santa Cruz Evening News*, (April 5, 1938): p.3.

- "No Action Taken on Comfort Stations on Beach Front," *Santa Cruz Evening News*, (July 24, 1923): p.3.

- "Norbeck Returns to Position with Seaside Company," *Santa Cruz Evening News*, (April 17. 1930): p.5.

- "Noted Artist to Paint Here," *Santa Cruz Evening News*, (February 29, 1928): p.2.

- "Noted Colored Band Plays in S.C. Tonight," *Santa Cruz Evening News*, (November 28, 1936): p.6.

- "Now Open River Bathhouse," *Santa Cruz Evening News* advertisement, (June 21, 1928): p.10.

- "Oakland Man Makes First Airplane Landing on Santa Cruz Beach," *Santa Cruz Evening News*, (December 24, 1928): p.3.

- "Ocean Wave Rider Asks $44,580 for Fractured Bones," *Santa Cruz Evening News*, (December 27, 1935): p.7.

- "Official Program for Celebration of Fourth," *Santa Cruz Evening News*, (July 3, 1920): p.5.

- "Old Santa Cruz," *News and Notes from the Santa Cruz Historical Society*, (Number 16, & June 1960): p. 4.

- "On the Boardwalk: Decades of Thrills and Beauty," *SJ Mercury California Today Sunday Magazine*, (Oct 14, 1979):p. 16.

- "On the Third Week," *Santa Cruz Daily Surf*, (November 2, 1903): p.1.

- "One Day in San Francisco," *Santa Cruz Daily Surf*, (November 12, 1903): p.1.

- "Onward Again," *Santa Cruz Daily Surf*, (April 26, 1893).

- "Opening Day Proclamation," *Santa Cruz Daily Surf*, (May 29, 1916): p.1.

- "Orand Gift Promenade," *Santa Cruz Daily Surf*, (June 21, 1909): p.2.

- "Out of it," *Santa Cruz Daily Surf*, (April 22, 1916): p.1.

- "Over $15,000 Being Spent By the Casa del Rey on Improvements," *Santa Cruz Evening News*, (November 10, 1933): p.6.

- "Over $300,000 Project for Beach Front." *Santa Cruz Evening News*, (August 13, 1924): p.1.

- "Over 20,000 Visitors in Santa Cruz," *Santa Cruz Evening News*, (July 5, 1919): p.4.

- "Ownership of the Beach Lands," *Santa Cruz Daily Surf,* (April 1, 1913): p.1.

- "Pappas Charges Discrimination as Council Holds Up Bath Permit and Hints Condemnation," *Santa Cruz Evening News,* (May 13, 1926): p.8.

- "Pathe Cameraman Films Scenes on Beach at Casino," *Santa Cruz Evening News,* (July 2, 1924): p.3.

- "Permanent Directors," *Santa Cruz Daily Surf,* (April 5, 1916): p.1.

- "Permit for Casa del Rey Apartments," *Santa Cruz Evening News,* (April 15, 1926) p.1.

- "Permit to Erect Giant Dipper Is Granted by Council," *Santa Cruz Evening News,* (January 18, 1924): p.4.

- "Photos for Life's Party Taken at Standard Frolic," *Santa Cruz Evening News,* (September 18, 1937) p.1.

- "Pilfering at Natatorium," *Santa Cruz Sentinel,* (April 20, 1920): p.3.

- "Plane Drops Into the Bay," *Santa Cruz Evening News,* (August 6, 1924): p.1.

- "Plans Complete for Plunge Opening at Beach Saturday," *Santa Cruz Evening News,* (March 15, 1937): p.3.

- "Plans for New Beach Resort Are Approved," *Santa Cruz Evening News,* (May 31, 1930): p.8.

- "Plans Offered for Underpass to S.C. Beach," *Santa Cruz Evening News,* (March 4, 1935): p.2.

- "Pleased with Way Concessionaires Obey Health Law," *Santa Cruz Evening News,* (July 13, 1928): p.9.

- "Plunge Opening March 24 Will Inaugurate Season," *Santa Cruz Evening News,* (March 14, 1934): p.1.

- "Plunge Set for 6 Millionth Customer," *Santa Cruz Evening News,* (March, 1942).

- "Plunge Set For the 1943 Swim Season," *Santa Cruz Sentinel,* (March 26, 1943): p.4.

- "Post-War Plans for Monterey Bay Area Being Formulated," *Santa Cruz Sentinel,* (April 1, 1943): p.1.

- "Private Tents," *Santa Cruz Daily Surf,* (May 15, 1905): p.1.

- "Prof. Karnoh at the Casino," *Santa Cruz Daily Surf,* (June 17, 1917).

- "Propeller Parts in Air," *Santa Cruz Evening News,* (July 6, 1920) p. 5.

- "Proposed Week End Program of Entertainment," *Santa Cruz Daily Surf,* (December 12, 1908): p.1.

- "Public Meeting Reveals Condition of Great Beach Front Industry; Santa Cruzans on Directorate," *Santa Cruz Evening News,* (February 25, 1928): p.3.

- "Pyramid of Flowers for Mothers Day," *Santa Cruz Evening News,* (May 8, 1933): p.1.

- "Quarter of Million Folks Spend Fourth in City and Beach and Hill Resorts," *Santa Cruz Evening News,* (July 5, 1932): p.2.

- "Radio Phone Service Secured at Beach," *Santa Cruz Evening News,* (April 6, 1922): p.1.

- "Record Crowd Invades the City," *Santa Cruz Evening News,* (July 5,1922): p.1.

- "Record of Arrests Shows Some Speeding," *Santa Cruz Evening News,* (July 8, 1920): p. 6.

- "Red Wallace Was A Swimming Great," *Santa Cruz Sentinel,* (March 26, 1943): p.4.

- "Redecorating Jobs at Beach Progressing," *Santa Cruz Evening News,* "March 12, 1937): p.6.

- "Reorganization Notice," *Santa Cruz Daily Surf,* (September 14, 1906): p.1.

- "Restaurant to Have Glass Front," *Santa Cruz Daily Surf,* (October 1, 1904): p.7.

- "Riptide," *Santa Cruz Evening News,* (March 5, 1935): p.3.

- "S.C. Seaside Co Directors All Are Re-elected," *Santa Cruz Evening News,* (February 27, 1932): p.5.

- "Safety Problems for Beach Front," *Santa Cruz Evening News,* (April 12, 1921): p.3.

- "Salt Water Baths Opened to Public; Leased by Hanly," *Santa Cruz Evening News,* (October 21, 1926): p.9.

- "Sam Haberman Back in Former Beach Location," *Santa Cruz Evening News,* (June 24, 1926): p.10.

- "Samuel Leask advertisement," *Santa Cruz Evening News,* (July 14, 1926): p.3.

- "Sanitary Conditions to be Improved," *Santa Cruz Evening News*, (June 19,1923): p.4.

- "Santa Cruz Beach Boardwalk Beach News," *Santa Cruz Seaside Company, Santa Cruz, California*, (October 2001; Jan 2002).

- "Santa Cruz Beach Boardwalk Questionnaire to Local Residences in 1911," *S.P.R.R. Santa Cruziana. F869 S48.Q47*, (1911).

- "Santa Cruz Beach Co. Properties Inspected by Possible Buyers," *Santa Cruz Evening News*, (March 15, 1932): p.3.

- "Santa Cruz Beach Cottage and Tent City Corporation," (September 13, 1904): p.1.

- "Santa Cruz Beach Cottage and Tent City Corporation," *Santa Cruz Daily Surf*, (October 3, 1904): p.1.

- "Santa Cruz Beach Cottage and Tent City Corporation," *Santa Cruz Daily Surf*, (October 26, 1903): p.1.

- "Santa Cruz Boardwalk a Survivor, Boardwalk Blends Old With New, Boardwalk has Tons of Memorabilia," *Santa Cruz Sentinel*, (January 29, 1991).

- "Santa Cruz Casino," *Santa Cruz Daily Surf*, (November 10, 1906): p.1.

- "Santa Cruz Company," *Santa Cruz Daily Surf*, (Sep 15, 1906): p.3.

- "Santa Cruz has a Long History of Convention Business," *San Jose Mercury News*, (January 26, 1993): p.1B.

- "Santa Cruz Is Drab, Backwards Rotary Hears," *Santa Cruz Evening News*, (March 18, 1927): p.1.

- "Santa Cruz Loses an Attraction," *Santa Cruz Sentinel*, (April 30, 1975): p.37.

- "Santa Cruz Seaside Company," *Santa Cruz Daily Surf*, (February 15, 1916): p.1.

- "Santa Cruz Sentinel Local News Index, 1940 -1943," *Friends of the Library, Santa Cruz, California*, (2002).

- "Santa Cruz Venetian Water Carnival," *The Traveler, San Francisco*, (1895).

- "Santa Cruzans May Manage the Casino," *Santa Cruz Daily Surf*, (May 26, 1914): p. 8.

- "Saturday Evening," *Santa Cruz Daily Surf*, (June 16, 1914): p.1.

- "SC Roller-coaster Getting a Facelift," *Santa Cruz Sentinel*, (January 2, 1976).

- "Scenic Grotto," *Santa Cruz Daily Surf*, (June 30, 1906): p. 1.

- "Seaside Co. Files Quiet Title Suit," *Santa Cruz Evening News*, (September 29, 1931): p.1.

- "Seaside Co. Pledges Aid to Navy Fund," *Santa Cruz Sentinel*, (May 3, 1942): p.5.

- "Seaside Co. Prepares Beach Front Fight," *Santa Cruz Evening News*, (August 29, 1930): p.1.

- "Seaside Co. Purchases S.P. Tract," *Santa Cruz Evening News*, (September 23, 1926): p.7.

- "Seaside Co. Will Construct at $1,000 Cost," *Santa Cruz Evening News*, (August 4, 1941): p.8.

- "Seaside Company Appoints Three to Director Board," *Santa Cruz Evening News*, (February 27, 1937): p.5.

- "Seaside Company Buys Solid Ocean Front Block," *Santa Cruz Evening News*, (September 16, 1925): p.1.

- "Seaside Company Commences Extension of Boardwalk to Kay Street on San Lorenzo," *Santa Cruz Evening News*, (July 15, 1926): p.9.

- "Seaside Company Embarks On Biggest Improvement Program Undertaken In Last 12 Years," *Santa Cruz Sentinel*, (January 21, 1940): p.1.

- "Seaside Company Reports 1934 Operating Profit," *Santa Cruz Evening News*, (February 25, 1935): p.1.

- "Seaside Damage Suit is Settled," *Santa Cruz Evening News*, (September 18, 1936): p.6.

- "Season At The Beach Formally Closed Sunday," *Santa Cruz Evening News*, (October 11, 1938): p.3.

- "Skating Fun in the Old Rink at Beach," *Santa Cruz Evening News*, (January 17, 1929): p.7.

- "Skee Roll is Newest Sport at Boardwalk," *Santa Cruz Evening News*, (March 26, 1935)": p.6.

- "Social," *Santa Cruz Sentinel*, (July 4, 1919): p. 4.

- "Southern Pacific to Fight Esplanade Paving Project," *Santa Cruz Evening News*, (May 23, 1927): p.2.

- "Special Train of Ohio Folks is Here Today," *Santa Cruz Evening News*, (August 13, 1932): p.2.

- "SSCBC&TC," *Santa Cruz Daily Surf*, (October 27, 1903) p.1.

- "Stagnaro and Beverino Seek Pleasure Pier," *Santa Cruz Evening News*, (July 29, 1934): p.10.

- "Stock Takers," *Santa Cruz Daily Surf*, (October 17, 1903): p.1.

- "Stratosphere Dive Is Featured For Tonite's Beach Water Carnival," *Santa Cruz Sentinel*, (June 7, 1941): p.5.

- "Structures to Overlook Ocean," *Santa Cruz Evening News*, (November 5, 1925): p.1.

- "Submarine Flotilla Arrives Here from San Pedro to Participate in Celebration of Navy Day," *Santa Cruz Evening News*, (October 27, 1922): p.1.

- "Subscribers and Subscriptions," *Santa Cruz Daily Surf*, (November 24, 1903): p.1.

- "Subscriptions, Estimates, and Contract," *Santa Cruz Daily Surf*, (November 19, 1903): p.1.

- "Sues Seaside Co. for $10,000 For Hurts on Chute," *Santa Cruz Evening News*, (December 26, 1930): p.1.

- "Suit Faces Seaside Firm," *Santa Cruz Sentinel*, (June 12, 1941): p.1.

- "Summer Rush on Beach Front," *Santa Cruz Morning News*, (June 21, 1921): p.6.

- "Swanton Pledges S.C. Cleanup," *Santa Cruz Evening News*, (May 23, 1932): p.1.

- "Swimming Plays Big Role In The War," *Santa Cruz Sentinel*, (March 26, 1943): p.4.

- "Tanker Off Monterey Bay," *Santa Cruz Evening News*, (December 21, 1941): p.1.

- "Tearing Down the Hot Baths," *Santa Cruz Daily Surf*, (January 20, 1904): p.5.

- "Texas Capitalist Views Buying Casa del Rey," *Santa Cruz Evening News*, (December 17, 1930): p.1.

- "The Board Walk," *Santa Cruz Daily Surf*, (July 23, 1907) p.2.

- "The Casino Fountain," *Santa Cruz Daily Surf*, (June 4, 1908): p.1.

- "The Fleet Will Stop At Santa Cruz," *Santa Cruz Daily Surf,* (March 11, 1908): p.1.
- "The Giant Dipper," *Santa Cruz Evening News,* (May 15, 1924): p.10, advertisement.
- "The History of Swimming Told Before Women's Luncheon Club by W. Littlefield, Plunge Head," *Santa Cruz Evening News,* (September 23, 1937): p.4.
- "The New Casino," *Santa Cruz Daily Surf,* (Sep 15, 1906): p.1.
- "The Opening," *Santa Cruz Daily Surf,* (June 6, 1904): p.7.
- "The Plunge Baths," *Santa Cruz Daily Surf,* (July 6, 1906) p.4.
- "The Santa Cruz Baths," *Santa Cruz Daily Surf,* (March 27, 1893).
- "The Season Is Opened," *Santa Cruz Daily Surf,* (June 10, 1912): p.1.
- :The Swimming Baths," *Santa Cruz Daily Surf,* (March 28, 1893).
- "The Swimming Baths," *Santa Cruz Daily Surf,* (March 29, 1893).
- "The Water Front," *Santa Cruz Daily Surf,* (July 1, 1918): p.3.
- "The Weekend Crowd," *Santa Cruz Daily Surf,* (May 21, 1917): p.1.
- "This Week," *Santa Cruz Daily Surf,* (October 12, 1903): p.2.
- "Thompson Suggests that Work of Mary Jane Hanly in Cases of Emergency be Remunerated," *Santa Cruz Evening News,* (August 5, 1926): p.5.
- "Three Day Program At Beach Set," *Santa Cruz Evening News,* (September 1, 1934): p.1.
- "Tidings from Headquarters," *Santa Cruz Daily Surf,* (October 19, 1903): p.1.
- "Timely Topics," *Santa Cruz Sentinel,* (June 6, 1919): p.3.
- "Title Expert Holds City Has No Title to Disputed Beach, In Opinion of Seaside Company," *Santa Cruz Evening News,* (May 19, 1930): p.2.
- "To Run Tent City Restaurant," *Santa Cruz Daily Surf,* (February 18,1905): p.8.
- "Too Much Makeup, Too Much Skin," *San Jose Mercury News,* (June 7, 1994): p. 1B.
- "Traffic Thru City Hits 26 Cars A Minute," (August 31, 1941): p.1.
- "Trained Fleas on Board Walk," *Santa Cruz Evening News,* (May 25, 1927(): p.10.

- "Transaction of Great Importance to Santa Cruz," *Santa Cruz Sentinel,* (May 28, 1914): p.1.

- "Trial of Suit Against Beach Firm Launched" *Santa Cruz Evening News,* (October 13, 1937): p.2.

- "Troyers, Lessees of Casa Del Rey Tell Their Plan," *Santa Cruz Evening News,* (April 4, 1932): p.4.

- "Two Big Dance Orchestras to be at Casino," *Santa Cruz Evening News,* (April 6, 1935): p.2.

- "Two Gala Events Set For Beach Next Saturday," *Santa Cruz Evening News,* (May 3, 1933): p.2.

- "U.S. Cruiser Ends 2 Day Stay Here," *Santa Cruz Evening News,* (November 12, 1932): p.1.

- "Uncle Sam's Giant Sea Fighter here," *Santa Cruz Evening News,* (July 2, 1928): p.2.

- "Universal to Exhibit Films in S.C. Hall," *Santa Cruz Evening News,* (September 26, 1936): p.1.

- "Vacation Official Santa Cruz Beach Front Amusement Information," *Santa Cruz Evening News,* (August 5 and 12, 1924): p.10.

- "Vacation Plan Here By Cornick," *Santa Cruz Sentinel,* (April 14, 1942): p.1.

- "Vacation. Advertisement," *Santa Cruz Evening News,* (June 25, 1925): p.12; (June 30, 1925): p. 10; (July 2, 1925): p.10; (June 26, 1926): p.10; (July 1, 1926): p.12; (July 7, 1926): p.8, (August 17, 1926): p.9.

- "Vote Landslide Sweeps Fred W. Swanton Into Mayor's Chair At First Election," *Santa Cruz Evening News,* (May 4, 1927): p.1.

- "Waldo Coleman Sells Control Of Seaside Co," *Santa Cruz Sentinel,* (October 16, 1943): p.1.

- "Water Carnival was Social Event of the Season in 1890," *San Jose Mercury News,* (Mary 9, 1993): p. B.

- "Water Front," *Santa Cruz Evening News,* (February 14, 1923): p.6.

- "Water Front," *Santa Cruz Daily Surf,* (June 18, 1904): p.1.

- "Waterfront," *Santa Cruz Evening News,* (January 1): p.1; (May 13): p.3; (May 27): p.9; (May 30, 1927): p.6.

- "Waterman-Goebel Beach Building Again Discussed," *Santa Cruz Evening News,* (March 1, 1935): p.7.

- "Weekend Travel Continues Lively," *Santa Cruz Evening News*, (May 1, 1922): p.6.

- "What are City's Rights at Beach" Asks the Mayor," *Santa Cruz Evening News*, (July 13, 1923): p.1.

- "What Shall Be," *Santa Cruz Daily Surf*, (August 7, 1906): p.2.

- "When Tourists Came for 'The Merry Buffeting of the Waves," *Santa Cruz Sentinel*, (July 7, 1963).

- "Who Owns the Water Front?," *Santa Cruz Daily Surf*, (June 30, 1911): p.3.

- "Wind and Waves Strike Santa Cruz Shore," *Santa Cruz Evening News*, "February 12, 1926"): p.1.

- "Woman Tells of Accident in Testimony," *Santa Cruz Evening News*, (September 16, 1936): p.2.

- "Work Started on Board Walk at River Bank," *Santa Cruz Evening News*, (April 11, 1933): p.5.

- "Work Starts on Changes as Casa del Rey Hotel," *Santa Cruz Evening News*, (October 10, 1929): p.5.

- "Would Build New Scenic Railway," *Santa Cruz Evening News*, (October 30, 1923): p.1.

- "Would Have Stock in Beach Company Owned by the People of Santa Cruz," *Santa Cruz Evening News*, (June 22, 1926): p.1.

- "Youth Drowns in Crowded Beach Plunge," *Santa Cruz Evening News*, (April 14, 1937): p.1.

INTERVIEWS AND OTHER ASSISTANCE

This book would not have happened without the invaluable assistance from:

Rita Bottoms

University of California, Santa Cruz, former director of the Special Collections Library. This is truly a superior library that has preserved many of the finest historical records of our past.

Sarah A. Bunnett

Chairperson of the Friends of the Santa Cruz Public Library. The Friends are indexing old Santa Cruz. This is a huge amount of work by lots of people.

Jon Covello

Covello & Covello Photography. They have a good collection of old and more current historical photographs

Gretchen Dempewolf

Librarian Assistant, Special Collections, McHenry Library, University of California, Santa Cruz

Rachel McKay

Santa Cruz Art and History Museum Archivist. This library is growing in importance as an authoritative place to find source documents about the city.

Frank Perry

Excellent Santa Cruz historian and author.

Paul Stubbs

Librarian Assistant, Special Collections, McHenry Library, University of California, Santa Cruz. Paul was exceptionally helpful in finding source materials.

Carolyn Swift

Capitola History Museum. Historian, writer, very knowledgeable person about local history.

Researchers Anonymous

This group of people interested in local history meets monthly at the Santa Cruz Art and History Museum and was of great help in researching material for this book.

Celeste Trimble

Librarian Assistant, Special Collections, McHenry Library, University of California, Santa Cruz.

Harold J. van Gorder

Harold is a 102 year-old resident of Santa Cruz, excellent historian, former Boardwalk employee, and really nice man. He provided many of the photographs in this book from his personal collection and told lots of great stories. He even proofread it for us. Thanks Harold!

And a special thanks to proof readers: John Beal, Kathy Beal, Ralph Beal, Jorja Latham, and Harold J. van Gorder!

Index

The Authors

Chandra Moira Beal

Chandra Moira Beal is a freelance writer in Austin, Texas. She grew up in Santa Cruz, California going to the Boardwalk. Chandra is the author of *Splash Across Texas! The Definitive Guide to Swimming in Central Texas*, and has published hundreds of magazine articles. She is also a registered massage therapist and body worker, and volunteers with many community organizations.

To learn more, visit www.beal-net.com/laluna.

Richard Beal

Richard A. Beal is semi-retired after a successful business management career in Silicon Valley at places like Apple Computer and Stanford University. He was a Vice President at the Internet pioneering company Netscape. Today he rides horses and does cattle work; sells historic cowboy buckles on the internet (www.bealscowboybuckles.com); is on the Board of Directors for the University of California Santa Cruz's Friends of the Long Marine Laboratory and the Richard and Kathy Beal Family Fund; and finds time to research and write local history books. Richard and wife Kathy live in Aptos, California. To learn more, visit www.beal-net.com/richard.

How to Order This Book

You can order this book from any bookstore (tell them you want ISBN 0-9629974-2-0), from amazon.com, or directly from the publisher at:

PO Box 33189
Austin, Texas 78764
Fax: 775.305.2161
E-mail: la-luna@att.net

The single copy price, direct from the publisher, is $19.99, plus $4.50 for shipping. Texas residents need to add $2.00 to cover sales tax.

Please include the address where you want it sent and a daytime phone number in case there are any questions.

Splash Across Texas! The Definitive Guide to Swimming in Central Texas. Chandra Moira Beal, La Luna Publishing, ISBN 0967160405, $16.95 plus $4.50 for shipping. Texas residents need to add $1.40 to cover sales tax.

Highway 17: The Road to Santa Cruz. Richard A. Beal, The Pacific Group, ISBN 0962997404, $12.95 plus $4.50 for shipping. Texas residents need to add $1.44 to cover sales tax.